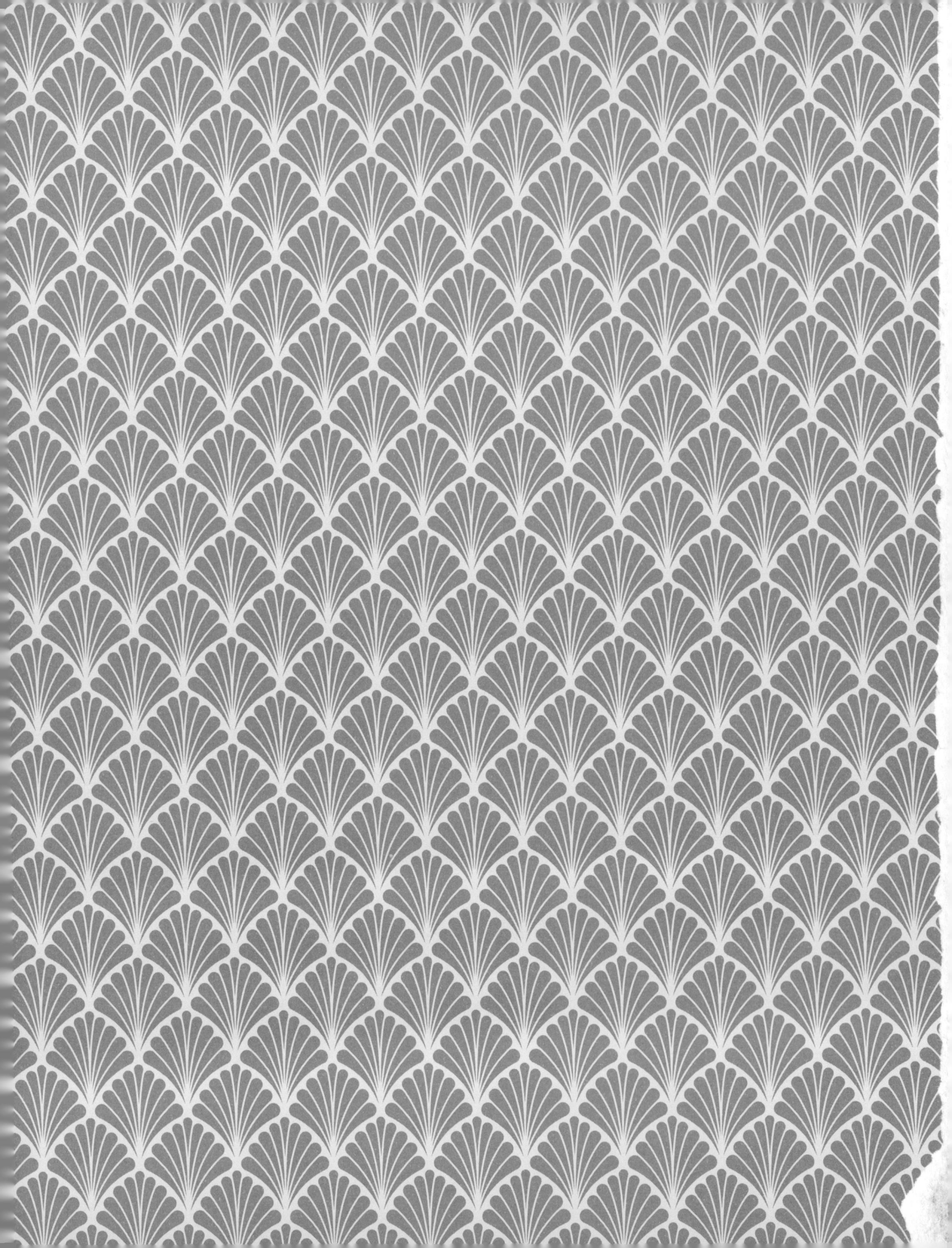

— THE —

FRENCH
BAKERY

COOKBOOK

THE FRENCH BAKERY COOKBOOK

13-Digit ISBN: 978-1-64643-446-6
10-Digit ISBN: 1-64643-446-3

This book may be ordered by mail from the publisher. Please include $5.99 for postage and handling. Please support your local bookseller first!

Books published by Cider Mill Press Book Publishers are available at special discounts for bulk purchases in the United States by corporations, institutions, and other organizations. For more information, please contact the publisher.

Cider Mill Press Book Publishers
"Where good books are ready for press"
501 Nelson Place
Nashville, Tennessee 37214
cidermillpress.com

Typography: Broadacre, Sofia Pro

Printed in Malaysia
24 25 26 27 28 OFF 5 4 3 2 1
First Edition

THE FRENCH BAKERY COOKBOOK

OVER 85 AUTHENTIC RECIPES THAT BRING
THE BOULANGERIE INTO YOUR HOME

KIMBERLY ZERKEL

CIDER MILL PRESS

BOOK PUBLISHERS

CONTENTS

THE ALLURE OF THE FRENCH BAKERY

In American cities, the French bakery is best understood on any given Saturday morning. From San Francisco to New York and many metropolitan areas in between, steady lines have been forming for decades now outside of French-style bread and pastry shops. The clientele is decidedly sophisticated and adult, although they await their weekend treats with the same anticipation as children looking forward to cereal and Saturday-morning cartoons. The majority of these folks would balk at the Burger King Croissan'wich. But they are content to wait for hours at a time for *pain au jambon*.

And who can blame them?

Of all the cultural contributions France has made to the world, their cuisine might be considered the greatest. Perhaps this is why strict laws apply to, say, which blue cheeses get to be named Roquefort, why Champagne—not prosecco—will always be poured at the most elegant of soirées, and why the French baguette has been dubbed by UNESCO as part of "the intangible cultural heritage of humanity." But out of all the gastronomical contributions the French have made, there is perhaps none so universally beloved as their bread and pastries.

Over the decades, lines to a French bakery have spread from the most cosmopolitan areas around the globe to smaller towns and cities the world over. Most countries have their own specialty breads, breakfast goods, and sweet treats, but they somehow haven't fended off the cries for buttery and rich *pain au chocolat*, light-as-air éclairs, or baguettes to be consumed for breakfast, lunch, and dinner. Even with the convenience of sliced sandwich bread and frozen-aisle baked goods, the clamor for French bakeries continues to rise. And now that social media has dissolved former borders and brought everything from Instagram posts about cronuts to TikTok videos on chocolate sculpting, the demand for this culinary art form has exploded.

I'm reminded of this as I line up at my town's French bakery here in the Ozarks. The weekend croissant I indulge in is a small reminder of my days of studying and working in Paris in my twenties. But the offerings that our local baker dishes out mean so much to those waiting alongside me. In a town that once lived on Wonder Bread, my fellow Midwesterners are now asking for *kouign-amann*, *pain au raisin*, and *ficelle* to accompany dark-roast coffee from a French press or elaborate charcuterie boards. Their cravings go beyond any sort of postmodern critique of globalization one might be tempted to dole out. I prefer to believe this change is positive and speaks to a

desire to return to traditional fare and tried-and-true baking methods that have existed for generations. We want food made by artisans, not factories.

Yet as complex as many of our thoughts might become on the subject, for the French, there is nothing more closely linked with the sweetness and simplicity of childhood than bread and pastries. Marcel Proust's more than four thousand pages of *In Search of Lost Time* start with the childhood memory of eating a madeleine. French goods, from candles to shower gel, are perfumed with orange blossom to replicate the scent of crêpes and other childhood treats infused with the extract. (Orange blossom is to the French what the smell of chocolate chip cookies is to Americans.) Adults across France still pause between 4 and 5 p.m. for tea and some form of cake or pastry, explaining that *le goûter, c'est sacré*—snack time is sacred.

The French don't like to wait in line for most things, but like their American counterparts, they will happily queue up at a bakery for good bread and croissants. With bread being a staple of the French diet, the bakery acts as the great equalizer. Sure, certain households send the nanny out to fetch daily loaves or weekend *viennoiseries* instead of picking them up themselves. But all must show fidelity to the neighborhood baker. No substitutions will do—a hard lesson to learn every August when these *maîtres artisans* close down shop for their yearly summer holiday.

Stroll the streets of Paris for proof of this fidelity. In each of the city's twenty arrondissements, you'll pass by many a local bakery with a line that spills out onto the sidewalk. It will be populated by little old ladies pulling shopping trolleys, stylish Parisians with organic produce-filled baskets, businesspeo-

ple checking their phones as they wait to grab their daily sandwich, and parents promising children that they'll receive the coveted first bite of baguette soon enough.

For them, this isn't indulgence. It's a way of life.

What Defines a French Bakery?

In English, the word "bakery" has been treated as an umbrella term for any establishment serving the likes of sourdough, blueberry muffins, cinnamon rolls, and tall, frosting-covered cakes. But for the French, each offering is distinctive and specialized enough to deserve its own name. These distinctions often come down to one simple thing: dough.

Boulangerie refers to a shop that specializes in bread. Although one can find baguettes in nearly every boulangerie across France, the name comes from *boule*, a round, country-style loaf that is similar in appearance to sourdough. For the *boulanger*, or baker, their area of expertise will always be in making bread dough.

Viennoiserie often goes hand in hand with a French bakery, as it pertains to other products that are not bread (such as brioche and croissants) but that are made through a similar technique, or with nearly identical dough. It's rare to find a bakery that sells one without the other. But while bread is considered essential, viennoiseries like pain au chocolat (chocolate croissant), *chaussons aux pommes* (apple turnover), and *palmiers* (elephant ears) are considered decadent—even though some indulge in viennoiseries every single day.

Pâtisserie is a pastry shop specializing in cakes and desserts. A *chef patissier* worth their salt (or sugar, in this case) has mastered the five principal doughs, including *pâte brisée* (pie dough), *pâte sablée* (shortcrust pastry), *pâte feuilletée* (flaky or puff pastry), *pâte à choux* (choux pastry), and *pâte phyllo* (phyllo

pastry). To these, an endless number of icings, glazes, creams, and fillings can be added. It is not entirely uncommon to find a bakery that sells bread, viennoiserie, and pastry all at once. But it's not uncommon either to find specially pastry shops that produce only sugary concoctions without a single loaf of bread in sight.

Finally, there are *chocolateries* and *confiseries*, chocolate shops and candy shops, that exist either on their own or inside boulangerie-viennoiserie-pâtisserie shops. French children leaving school might stop by for a croissant or *pain au lait* as well as a handful of gummy crocodiles (more sought-after than gummy bears) for their afternoon snack—although the health-conscious French would likely limit this to special occasions. A couple throwing a dinner party might set out to buy bread but also pick up chocolates or even homemade marshmallows at the same spot to accompany post-dinner coffee and digestifs.

The rule here is that all of these specialities might live under the same roof, but there's no guarantee. The only way to be sure is to carefully read the signage—or pop your head inside for a closer look.

Bread

The French are not generally known as humble people (a phrase they'd not be pleased to hear coming from an American). But even they have to admit that they didn't *invent* bread. There is evidence that prehistoric man was making loaves as far back as thirty thousand years ago. Ancient Egyptians enjoyed date, fig, and honey bread. Each country and culture in

the Mediterranean Basin has survived on its distinctive take on bread for millennia now.

France began consuming bread regularly in the Middle Ages, when it often replaced cutlery and was used to push food or sop up sauce. It could even be used as a plate itself. Medieval bakers created enormous *miches* (loaves) that could be sliced thickly, laid on the table, and used as the carrier for whatever was being served that evening.

The availability of bread in France starting at that period and for centuries to come symbolized stability and prosperity. The lack of bread sent panic and rumors of famine and revolt throughout the country. Bread was also at the center of religious life, particularly for Catholics, who consumed bread at Communion.

Fast-forward to the twentieth century, and bread production was greatly affected by two world wars that took place on French soil. During World War II in particular, food shortages led to the use of filler ingredients like soy flour. After the war, when wheat flour became abundant again, mass production of bread took off. Using fillers and cheap ingredients to make and sell as much bread as possible, and as cheaply as possible, helped meet the demand of new consumers who shopped for bread at the supermarket instead of the local bakery.

The French have never been ones to buck tradition, however. After decades of debate, *Le Decré Pain* (the Bread Decree) was passed in 1993, stating that traditional baguettes, or *pain de tradition française*, must be made on-site in the bakery that sells them. And they can only contain carefully measured-out flour, water, yeast, and salt, nothing more. Loaves of sandwich bread containing fillers still exist in large supermarket chains but can never claim to be traditional French bread, according to the government.

For many consumers, the quality of bread is recognizable by the sound it produces: a crackle when you squeeze a baguette or a hollow knock when you tap on the bottom of a round loaf. Bread should be full of pockets of air and, despite its simple list of ingredients, taste slightly salty, sweet, and buttery at the same time.

There are more than eighty different types of bread in France, each type unique to a specific region. There is *pain plié* in Brittany, literally "folded bread," as well as *pain tordu* in Midi, "twisted bread." The most famous loaf, the baguette, was invented in Paris.

Bread is more than just an essential form of calorie intake, it's a cornerstone of French culture. It is eaten as a *tartine* (piece of toast) for breakfast each morning (most save croissants for the weekend or as a snack). It is used to make sandwiches or served on the side of a salad at lunchtime. And it soaks up sauce or accompanies a cheese plate every night at dinner. That's how French bakers are able to sell approximately ten billion—yes, billion—baguettes a year.

Bread is so crucial to French society that its absence led in part to the French Revolution. Although Marie Antoinette, upon learning that there were bread shortages across the country, never said, "Let them eat cake," the shortage of bread itself was enough to send French citizens into revolt. It's for this reason that the price of a baguette is still discussed in French politics the same way the price of a gallon of milk or a tank of gas is talked about in the United States.

Viennoiserie

If ever there was a Venn diagram of the things both French speakers and bakers the world over know with absolute certainty, the overlap would consist of one simple fact: what quite a

few people mistake for pastry is actually viennoiserie. Tourists visiting France often flock to bakeries in search of what they would consider to be breakfast pastries. But the dough and technique used there differentiate them from the rest.

Viennoiserie refers to products made by a baker where the technique is similar to that of bread making. But the ingredients in viennoiserie make each offering slightly richer or sweeter, which is why they're often confused with dessert-like pastries. Viennoiserie relies on eggs, butter, milk, cream, and sugar for that extra bit of goodness so many know and love. Because croissants, pain au chocolat, pain au raisin, and brioche are also made of fermented dough, they are classified as a baker's area of expertise.

The name *viennoiserie* comes to us from August Zang, who opened Boulangerie Viennoise in Paris in 1839 at 92, rue de Richelieu, in the heart of the French capital. The idea was to serve baked goods similar to those in his hometown of Vienna. By the late 1800s, *pâtisseries viennoises* was being used in French to describe the croissants and other Viennoise-inspired fare being served around the city. Parisian bakers put their own spin on each recipe by introducing the use of flaky pastry into each bake, bridging the gap between what was served then and what we know to be viennoiserie today.

Viennoiserie is perfect for a decadent breakfast or an afternoon treat—but never for dessert. Which is perhaps why you would never expect to indulge in pain au raisin at the end of a dinner party. Knowing this—when and where certain baked goods are eaten—is one way of remembering the difference between viennoiserie and patisserie for those outside the Francophone/pastry chef realm.

Pastry

The French didn't invent bread, but they did invent dessert. The word itself derives from the French verb *desservir*, which means to clear the table. By the seventeenth century, French aristocracy began referring to the act of clearing off dishes and changing out napkins for the final fruit course as *dessert*, and the word soon caught on among the bourgeoisie.

Before the new vocabulary word became all the rage, there was (and still is) *entremets*, interval dishes that could be savory or sweet and served as a type of palate cleanser between other courses. France's earliest pastries and confections, then called *oublies*, came to life from this tradition in 1270 thanks to the country's first official pastry chef, Régnaut-Barbon.

Most early desserts that went beyond simply laying out a platter of fruit, cheese, and nuts involved jams and preserves, marzipan, and even rustic cookies. Over time, visually elegant desserts and pastries became the fashion, and having a decorative dessert spread was a must for aristocratic hosting. Well into the nineteenth century, well-to-do families were expected to have a spectacular dessert table for guests, such as the castle-shaped cake, jam lakes, and hazelnut boats described in Gustave Flaubert's *Madame Bovary*. Two world wars in the twentieth century obviously stifled this tradition as shortages of every kind, including sugar, made dessert a rarity. Today, the French are renowned for their sweet confections like macarons, éclairs, mousse, and crème brûlée.

If bread and viennoiserie are clearly defined in the French language, however, pastry gets a little murky. One might be tempted to say that a pastry chef is responsible for "everything else": cakes, pies, cream-based

tarts, cookies, chocolates, sweets, or even ice cream during the summer months. Their talents can be on full display in both a pastry shop and a restaurant. Some of their recipes can be easily replicated at home. (Most French households have a *moelleux au chocolat*, or molten chocolate cake, recipe memorized for any given birthday party.) Others are too fussy to be bothered with. (Why even attempt to make homemade phyllo dough when you can buy it ready-made at almost any grocery store?) But one thing is certain: the end result is a thing of dreams.

While bread is considered essential to survival, pastry is considered essential to thriving. And there is a pastry concoction for nearly every moment of the year. The French start off January by slicing into *galettes des rois*, the original "King Cake" made from puff pastry and frangipane. They end the year by devouring candied chestnuts and citrus-based desserts all December long before finally cutting into a *bûche de Noël*, or yuletide log cake, for Christmas.

French Bread and Pastries Today

Once, you could sit down with French exchange students or expats and find a common thread that went beyond shared language and origin. Almost all shared a general dissatisfaction with bread and bakes from other countries, particularly the United States. Whether or not they had any sort of culinary background, French citizens living abroad knew good bread and pastries like they knew the words to "La Marseillaise." These recipes were something they grew up with and ate regularly, if not daily. Their dissatisfaction with American sliced bread or sugary-sweet cakes stemmed

from a long lineage of *savoir-faire* and *savoir-vivre*, the French terms for knowing how to do everything, including living, just right.

But the lines outside bakeries today are not necessarily for star bakers hailing from France. And the fare served inside is no longer limited to traditional recipes but includes cultural influences and ingredients from all over the world. In the United States, there is a growing number of artisanal bakeries inspired by French boulangeries-pâtisseries. This rise has coincided with that of celebrity chefs, as well as a piqued interest in food culture in general. Baguettes, rustic loaves, and French-style pastries are now being served by a new generation of bakers and pastry chefs across North America, many of which are highlighted throughout this book.

This generation has already been marked by a significant change. At the start of the Covid-19 pandemic, many bakers and pastry chefs realized that they were able to adapt to restaurant and bakery closures through "cottage baking," or serving a limited amount of bread and treats from their home or via delivery. So, even as crowds have now returned to gathering every weekend for their favorite loaves and flaky pastries, many have found they can sell bread, cookies, or croissants without necessarily having a brick-and-mortar storefront. These artisans will be featured here as well.

They hope, as I do, that you will not only continue to love the experience of going out and enjoying your favorite French bakeries in person but that you'll also learn to recreate some of these classic bread, viennoiserie, and pastry recipes at home.

After all, weekends are too short to always be waiting in line.

CHAPTER 1

LE PAIN

BREAD

Bread can be (and often is) consumed at every meal in
France. Although low-carb crazes have come and gone,
bread will always be the mainstay of the French diet. But
it's not only in France that French bread is celebrated.
The world over recognizes the hearty goodness of
freshly baked loaves and the delicious practicality
of France's most popular export, the baguette.

THE BAGUETTE

The baguette is the most familiar form of French bread, at least to those of us on the outside looking in. Its name comes from its distinctive shape. "Baguette" is a name given to a number of long, thin, stick-like items in French, from drumsticks to magic wands. (That's right, in the French translation of J. K. Rowling's work, Harry Potter wields une baguette magique.) It's that very shape that you'll find placed strategically at the center of a dinner table or poking out of rucksacks and grocery bags as you walk down the street.

Because it is one of France's most iconic foods, there are multiple myths behind the legend that is now the baguette. Some say that Napoleon Bonaparte commanded French bakers to create loaves that were easy for soldiers to carry. Considering that Napoleonic code still has a massive influence on French life, this is easy to believe. Others say it was necessary to find bread that was easy for Parisian workers to break by hand and eat on their lunch break. This was less about efficiency and more out of the desire to eliminate the need for knives and the bloody fights that came with them.

The most likely origin story says that the baguette was created in Paris at the turn of the twentieth century after an Austrian baker named August Zang brought steam ovens to the French capital. Zang is credited with bringing croissants and viennoiserie to Paris and just might be the father of the baguette as well. His steam ovens allowed the bread to expand into the light, airy concoction we now know today—and created the iconic crust that so many love.

In the 1920s, Zang's steam ovens proved to be a saving grace. A law was passed forbidding bakers to start their work before 4 a.m. This was partially due to noise complaints by those living above bakeries, but also to ensure better working conditions for those laboring in the bakeries. However, the pressure to produce bread cooked all the way through in time for the morning rush was immense. Wide, flat loaves took too long to bake, but long, thin loaves baked much faster, especially in steam ovens. When the breakfast crowd realized how easy it was to slice a baguette for a quick piece of toast or sandwich (or simply rip off a piece by hand), it caught on as the preferred way to start a morning.

France's Bread Decree applies most directly to the baguette. A tradition is shorthand for the original baguette made from only flour, yeast, salt, and water. All other baguettes will either include varied ingredients, such as whole grains, or differ slightly in method.

PAIN D'AVIGNON

15 Hinckley Road
Hyannis, MA 02601

Café d'Avignon locations in New York include the Essex Street Market, Dekalb Market Hall, Times Square, The Moxy Chelsea, The Moxy Lower East Side, The Moxy East Village, Plaza Food Hall, and, soon, Rockefeller Center.

In a journey that started in Belgrade amid the beginnings of war and continued in America, four friends tested their philosophy—that individuals should strive to pursue what they love—to the extreme. They began a new life and opened a tiny bakery together on Cape Cod. Working hectic, twenty-four-hour days while living together in a loft above their business and making it all up as they went along, the founders of Pain d'Avignon quickly became some of the first highly acclaimed purveyors of artisanal bread in the Northeast.

For thirty years, Pain d'Avignon has been pursuing excellence in the art of bread making inspired by the old-world methods while partnering with New York's top chefs to bring a five-star bread to our everyday life. As a baker who had an unorthodox bread education, Uliks Fehmiu has learned over time that practice and patience are the most important parts of the journey. Here he shares this important lesson with home bakers, along with five-star bread and pastry recipes, an accessible, step-by-step primer on mastering the fundamentals, and a tale of adventure from the iconic East Coast bakery.

Uliks Fehmiu is an actor, producer, and self-taught baker. He cofounded the Pain d'Avignon bakery with his friends Branislav Stamenkovic, Vojin Vujosevic, and Igor Ivanovic in 1992. Pain d'Avignon has been featured in *The Boston Globe*, *The Wall Street Journal*, *The New York Times*, *New York Magazine*, *Boston Magazine*, *Crain's Business*, *Wine Spectator*, *Cape Cod Life*, *Saveur*, *Eater*, *Edible Cape Cod*, and *Cape Cod Times*, among others. The journey of these friends, accompanied by recipes for their renowned bakes, are featured in their book, *The Pain d'Avignon Baking Book: A War, An Unlikely Bakery, and a Master Class in Bread*. For *The French Bakery Cookbook*, they share their classic baguette and kouign-amann recipes.

PAIN D'AVIGNON'S CLASSIC BAGUETTE

Yield: 3 baguettes

Pain d'Avignon shares their recipe for one of the world's most beloved bread recipes. Don't have a steam oven, the famous invention that made the baguette possible? The recipe calls for a few ice cubes in the oven to create steam—and the baguette's unforgettable golden crust.

325 g water (24°C/75°F)

150 g pâte fermentée (young levain)

500 g bread flour

14 g salt

0.15 g active dry yeast

25 g bassinage (drenching water)

1. Mix the dough by combining all of the ingredients in a stand mixer.

2. Fold: Bulk fermentation time is 2 hours. Stretch and fold the dough once after 1 hour.

3. Divide: Set a cutting board big enough to hold three loaves nearby. With a dough scraper, loosen the dough from the container. Flip the container over onto the work surface, being careful not to let the dough fold onto itself. (If it does fold onto itself, use the dough scraper to coax it apart.) Cut and weigh the dough into three 275 g pieces. You will make 3 baguettes, and the remaining dough will be used tomorrow as your pâte fermentée starter. Put the piece of starter dough in a container with a tight-fitting lid and refrigerate.

4. Pre-shape: Place the dough, seam-side down, on the resting board, cover with a kitchen towel, and set aside to rest in a warm (24°C/75°F), draft-free spot for 20 minutes.

5. Shape: Place a large linen towel or couche on a large cutting board or overturned half-sheet pan and coat liberally with dusting flour. Touch each piece of dough with your palm. If sticky, dust a handful of flour onto a clean work surface. If smooth and not at all tacky, skip the flour. With a dough scraper, flip each loaf from the board onto the work surface. With a long side facing you and with a gentle touch, partially press down

Continued...

the dough to even thickness with your palms. (Take care not to deflate it too much.) Lift the dough to prevent it from sticking to the work surface and gently stretch it before you put it back on the work surface. Working with one piece at a time, fold the top two-thirds of the dough onto itself, sealing the seam gently with your fingertips. Rotate the piece 180 degrees and repeat. Then fold the dough over itself lengthwise while pushing with your thumb inward along the seam and sealing it with the palm of your other hand. The dough should look like a stubby baguette. Using the palms of your hands, and with your thumbs set against the seam, roll the dough into a uniformly thick 12-inch-long tube, sealing the seams with your thumbs as you roll. Working from the center outward, use your palms to roll the tube out to a 15-inch-long baguette; you may need to do this once or twice. Taper the ends by applying pressure to the "tails" as you roll the dough away from you. Repeat with the remaining dough.

6. Proof: Using the dough scraper, loosen the loaves from the work surface and gently transfer them to the towel or couche, seam-side up, spacing them 2 inches apart. Make a pleat in the towel on either side of the loaves to create "walls" that will help the loaves retain their shape. Give each baguette a liberal dusting of flour by tapping the flour onto them through a sieve. Cover with a kitchen towel and set aside to proof in a warm (24°C/75°F), draft-free spot until the loaves have grown in height and expanded in volume, about 45 minutes. If any part of the seam is split, pinch it together with your fingers. Put the baguettes in the refrigerator for at least 1 hour or up to 12 hours.

7. Score and bake: About 30 minutes before you are ready to bake, prepare a sheet of parchment paper the same size as your baking stone and place it on the back of a sheet pan or on a baking peel. Position a rack in the center of the oven and place the stone on it. Preheat the oven to 260°C/500°F.

8. Gently transfer the baguettes from the couche to the parchment paper by sliding a flipping board underneath each and rolling them over onto the parchment so that they are seam-side down. Score the loaves with three vertical cuts on an angle spanning the length of the dough.

9. Wearing long, sturdy oven mitts and using the parchment like a sling, gently transfer the baguettes onto the stone (pull the oven rack out)—parchment and all. Throw one ice cube into each corner of the oven and close the door. Bake until golden all over, about 15 minutes, then open the door to let the steam out and bake until the crust is deep, dark golden and the ends of the baguette curve upward, 5 to 8 minutes more. Transfer to a wire rack to cool.

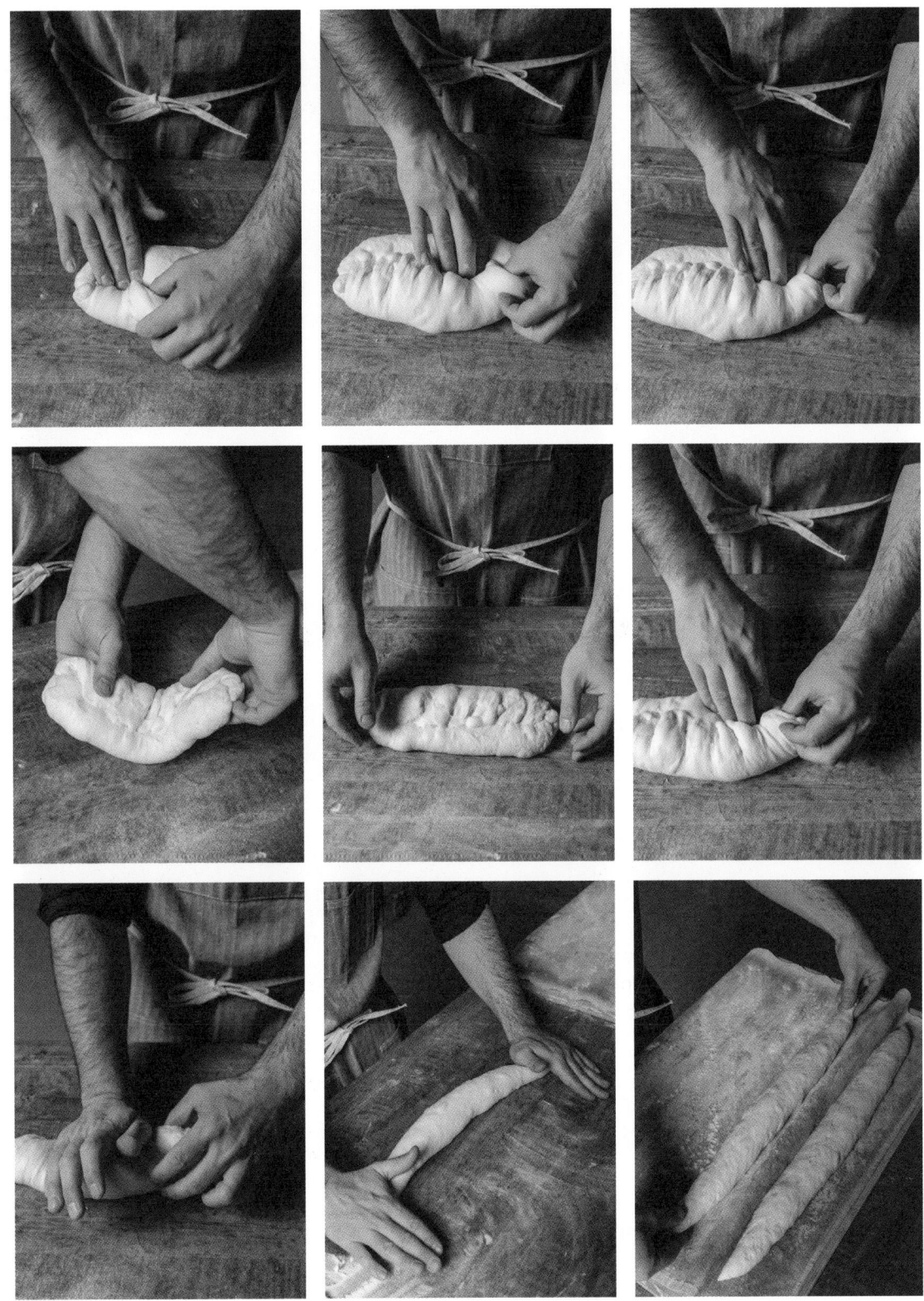

OTHER FRENCH BREADS

Even though the baguette is perhaps the most iconic form of French bread, there's a reason that the French bakery is not named une baguetterie. Before the baguette, there was—and always will be—la boule. The round boule is actually the more traditional or rustic form of French bread, despite it not having the same fame as its more slender cousin. The rules pertaining to round loaves aren't as strict as with baguettes. Different flours and yeasts can be used, and herbs and spices can be folded in for flavor. But a simple loaf, similar in flavor to sourdough, is what is preferred by the French, coming in second right after baguettes.

A boule keeps better than a baguette. The latter dries out within 24 to 48 hours if not properly stored. The thicker, rounder shape of a traditional loaf helps it stay moist for several days. But because it does not cut or rip apart by hand as easily as a baguette, it is better suited for home, while a baguette is practically made for a picnic.

Other varieties of bread include ficelle, a twisted ultra-thin cousin to the baguette that can be enhanced by the addition of olives, Gruyère, or lardons; fougasse, a favorite in the South of France that's similar to focaccia or pizza dough; *pain aux noix*, a specialty hailing from the Southwest that is made of whole wheat and walnuts; *pain de campagne*, a country loaf similar to sourdough; and *pain de mie*, the white or whole wheat loaf closest to American sliced bread. These varieties only scratch the surface when it comes to the vast array of assortments to be found in France's breadbasket.

SHINYA PAIN

41, rue des Trois Frères
Paris, France 75018

Having left Japan for France at the age of twenty, Shinya Inagaki is considered by many in Paris to be one of the capital's finest bakers to date. After working in multiple Parisian establishments such as Fermentation Générale, La Boulangerie du Nil, and Le Grenier à Pain, Chef Shinya made the decision to open his own rustic establishment in the heart of Montmartre. Shinya Pain is known for its simplicity; the dark walls are nearly bare, their charcoal color set off by amber-colored loaves of bread and speckled cookies and scones. Beyond a large oven and sacks of grain, the only other thing to catch a customer's attention is Inagaki's broad smile as he receives a steady stream of customers on the days he is open.

Shinya says that having his own location has given him the time to let the materials he works with take shape and transform in their own time. He works nearly every dough by hand and uses his own sourdough starter as well as flour made from heirloom grains. Terroir being as important in bread as it is in wine, he procures these flours from mills principally found around the Île-de-France region (Paris and its surrounding suburbs).

He says that, for him, sincerity and simplicity of ingredients are the most important, as well as a respect for the necessary time it takes to transform these "magnificent materials" into their own unique personality. In keeping with the rustic charm of his bakery, Chef Shinya posts the written menu of his daily offerings on Instagram, nothing more. He receives customers for only three hours, from 4:30 to 7:30 p.m., Thursday through Sunday.

PAIN DE MÉTEIL

The earthy flavor of Shinya's meslin bread comes from a combination of half whole wheat flour and rye. Although it can be eaten for any meal, and made both savory and sweet, this hearty loaf is ideal for accompanying soups or other hot meals enjoyed on a cold night.

250 g half whole wheat flour (T80)

250 g rye flour (T130)

10 g salt, preferably sea salt

420 mL water

120 g yeast

1. In a large mixing bowl, mix together the wheat and rye flours.

2. In another large mixing bowl, mix the water and salt.

3. Mix the flours with the yeast, and then add the salt water. Form the dough into a ball.

4. Cover the dough with a cloth and let it rest for 20 minutes, preferably in a 24°C/75°F atmosphere.

5. Knead the dough and then let it rest again under the cloth for another 20 minutes. Repeat this kneading and resting 3 more times.

6. Move the covered dough to the refrigerator and let it rest for 18 hours.

7. Bring it out of the refrigerator after 18 hours and let it rest for 40 minutes at room temperature.

8. Shape the dough into a ball, then let it rest for another 40 minutes.

9. During this last rest, preheat your oven to 250°C/480°F.

10. Take the ball and gently cut a cross over the top using a razor blade, if possible.

11. Right before putting it into the oven, lightly mist it with water from a spray bottle.

12. Let the bread bake for 10 minutes before turning the temperature down to 220°C/430°F. Let it continue to bake for 35 to 40 minutes longer.

LE TOLEDO

351 Mont-Royal Avenue E
Montreal, Quebec
H2T 1R1, Canada

Le Toledo opened in March 2019 and only a year later was voted best baguette in Montreal. Being the best was part of their mission from the start. The French-based team decided to open their bakery in Le Plateau, a Montreal neighborhood known for its culinary scene—and for its steep competition. Why bake bread next to some of the city's best bakeries and pastry shops? If they can make it there, they can make it anywhere, according to the team. And not making it would mean rethinking their dream. Luckily for us, their delicious offerings and wild success mean that we can enjoy their award-winning bakes for years to come.

LA MEULE

Le Toledo is a go-to destination for French-style loaves in Montreal. Here, they share their recipes for a large loaf (1,600 grams, or 3.5 pounds vs. lb./lbs. = search all and edit if consistency is desired.) of millstone bread that is the perfect accompaniment for most meals. Their advice? Make it into toast or an open-faced sandwich.

890 g organic stone-ground half whole wheat flour (T80)

775 g water

18 g salt

445 g hard leaven

45 g drenching water

1. Mix the flour and water together in a mixer for 3 minutes.

2. Let the dough rest for 1 hour.

3. Add the salt and hard leaven and continue to mix at low speed for 8 minutes.

4. Finish mixing at high speed for 1 minute.

5. Add the drenching water and mix at high speed for 1 more minute.

6. Let the dough rest for 1.5 hours.

7. Remove the dough and knead it using the slap-and-fold method: Turn the dough out onto your work surface and gently pick it up with your fingertips. Slap the dough down onto the surface and then fold the dough away from you as if you are tucking it underneath itself. Repeat this until the dough begins to smooth and hold its shape.

8. Let the dough rest for 45 minutes.

9. Begin to shape the dough into a boule: Lay the dough out in a pre-shaped and semi-flat circle, then pull the right and left sides ("wings") of the dough toward the middle. Then fold the top and bottom edges inward, making the dough look like an envelope. Place your hands underneath the dough and drag it toward you, rolling it and shaping it into a ball as you do so. Repeat this until the dough is smooth with no tears on the outside.

10. Let the dough rest in the refrigerator for 12 hours.

11. Bake at 240°C/450°F for 1 hour.

LE PAIN QUI TUE

A killer! Hence the name—Le Toledo's Killer Bread. Le Toledo serves slices of this hearty bread with a thick layer of peanut butter, making it the most decadent sweet-and-salty offering of their entire range of products.

11 g glucose

55 g granulated sugar

46 g whole hazelnuts

210 g organic stone-ground flour (T65)

146 g water

6 g yeast

42 g hard leaven

4 g salt

31 g drenching water

17 g honey

31 g olive oil

1. Make the caramel: mix the glucose and sugar together in a saucepan and bring to a boil until it thickens.

2. Add the hazelnuts to the hot caramel and let the mixture cool and harden on a sheet pan.

3. When the mixture has completely hardened, break it into small pieces with a hammer.

4. Begin making the dough by mixing the flour and water together; let the dough rest for 1 hour.

5. Add the yeast, hard leaven, and salt, then mix in a mixer on low for 8 minutes.

6. Add the drenching water, honey, and olive oil, then mix on high for 4 minutes.

7. Add the pieces of caramel and mix in by hand; transfer the dough to your work surface, knead, and then let rest at room temprature for 45 minutes.

8. Knead the dough once moreand then let the dough rest in the refrigerator for 12 hours.

9. Take the dough out of the refrigerator and shape it into a ball.

10. Wait 15 minutes, shape it into a ball once again, and let it rise for 1.5 hours.

11. Bake it at 250°C/480°F for 20 minutes.

HENDRICKX

100 E Walton Street
Chicago, IL 60611

Hendrickx is a Chicago-based Belgian bakery owned and operated by Chef Renaud Hendrickx. The bakery, which also serves light fare, is known for its artisanal breads, over thirteen flavors of croissants, and pastries. In July 2021 it was nominated as one of Chicago's best bakeries by *Time Out*. Chef Renaud and his team offer us two Belgian recipes that would be welcome in any French or European-style bakery: white chocolate bread and Brussels waffles.

PAIN AU CHOCOLAT BLANC

Yield: 2 loaves

This recipe calls for Callebaut white chocolate and yields approximately 2 small white breads, depending on the mold you use. The important thing is to fill the mold well and to let the bread rise. "Don't worry if the dough seems very liquid and sticks to your fingers. That is how it should be. That is why you need to work on a plastic sheet and use a good quantity of flour. The flour will serve as a rampart between fingers and dough. Also, the quicker you move the dough, the less your fingers will touch it. They will be protected by the flour. Have fun. Bon appétit!" —Chef Renaud Hendrickx

300 g flour

6 g dry yeast

Pinch salt

1 teaspoon cinnamon

40 g brown sugar

230 g water, at room temperature

1 egg

1 squirt orange extract

1 squirt vanilla extract

160 g white chocolate blocks

40 g pearl sugar

1. Combine flour, yeast, salt, and cinnamon in a large bowl. Gently toss brown sugar in with the dry ingredients.

2. Add room temperature water, egg, and extracts.

3. Stir with a wooden spoon until just combined and flour is hydrated.

4. Flour plastic sheet and sprinkle dough generously with flour.

5. Turn dough out onto plastic. It will be very sticky and soft.

6. Divide dough to fill your molds. Drop dough into buttered molds(s).

7. Push chunks of white chocolate into dough unevenly.

8. Sprinkle each loaf with pearl sugar and let rise for 15 minutes.

9. Bake for 19 to 24 minutes at 190°C/375°F until chocolate and pearl sugar are caramelized and golden.

DU PAIN ET DES IDÉES

34, rue Yves Toudic
Paris, France 75010

In a city that's known as a destination for both gourmands and budding philosophers, is it any wonder that Paris's most cherished bakery is named Du Pain et des Idées (DPDI)? The name translates to "bread and ideas," and both are on full display in what is considered the French capital's finest boulangerie.

The thoughtful attention to detail that has Parisians and tourists alike flocking to this 10th-arrondissement establishment starts with the building itself, located a stone's throw from the trendy Canal Saint-Martin. This address has been a bakery since 1875, and much of the decor remains untouched from that period, including painted glass ceilings and beveled mirrors. It's for this reason that DPDI is listed as one of the city's historical sites.

But it's what is inside each of the display cases that attracts all of the bakery's well-deserved attention. DPDI is known for its baguettes (which have a slight chestnut flavor to them), homemade pain des amis (trademarked by the bakery), orange blossom brioches, chocolate-pistachio escargot (a decadent take on the more wholesome pain au raisin), and fresh apple turnovers that are as delicious to the eye as they are to the tastebuds.

Owner and baker Christophe Vasseur is a self-taught artisan who left behind his career as a fashion industry salesperson in 2002 to pursue his dream of running an authentic Parisian bakery. The ideas that he wished to incorporate into his bakes revolved primarily around the quality of ingredients he and his team would use. They believe firmly in sourcing the best raw materials, directly from the producer if possible; on their website, they list milk from the Beaulieu Estate in nearby Seine-et-Marne as an example. They also use almost entirely organic materials. They consider their offerings to be both delicious and healthy and are proud to produce everything on-site.

For *The French Bakery Cookbook*, they have graciously contributed their recipes for milk bread and a chocolatey tartine. For more recipes, their book, *Pain de la terre à la table* ("bread from the earth to the table"), is available, as are classes with Christophe himself.

LE PAIN AU LAIT

This bread recipe is perfect for breakfast or a snack. However, you'll need to anticipate 30 hours to prepare it. Inspired by Sunday or feast-day bread in Brittany, this bread is a sweeter and more buttery version of the famous Paris bakery's home-made bread.

75 g granulated sugar

1 kg wheat flour, ideally organic type 65 (T65)

18 g salt

8 g fresh baker's yeast

500 to 650 g lukewarm milk (the necessary quantity will vary depending on the flour)

100 g butter, melted and lukewarm

Flour for the work surface

1 egg yolk (optional)

1. In a large bowl, combine the sugar, flour, salt, and yeast and then stir in the milk.

2. Once the flour is no longer visible, pour in the previously melted and cooled butter (like the milk, it should be lukewarm). If necessary, add the remaining milk to the dough.

3. Form a large ball of milk bread from all of the dough or roll the dough until it is 2 centimeters thick, then cut it into fun shapes using a cookie cutter or a knife. Individual milk bread loaves of approximately 10 centimeters in size should be baked for around 15 minutes at 180°C to 200°C/350°F to 400°F .

4. Before putting in the oven, dab the milk bread(s) with the egg yolk so that it/they will be golden brown.

5. For a variation at the end of the preparation, you can add chips of nougat or chocolate.

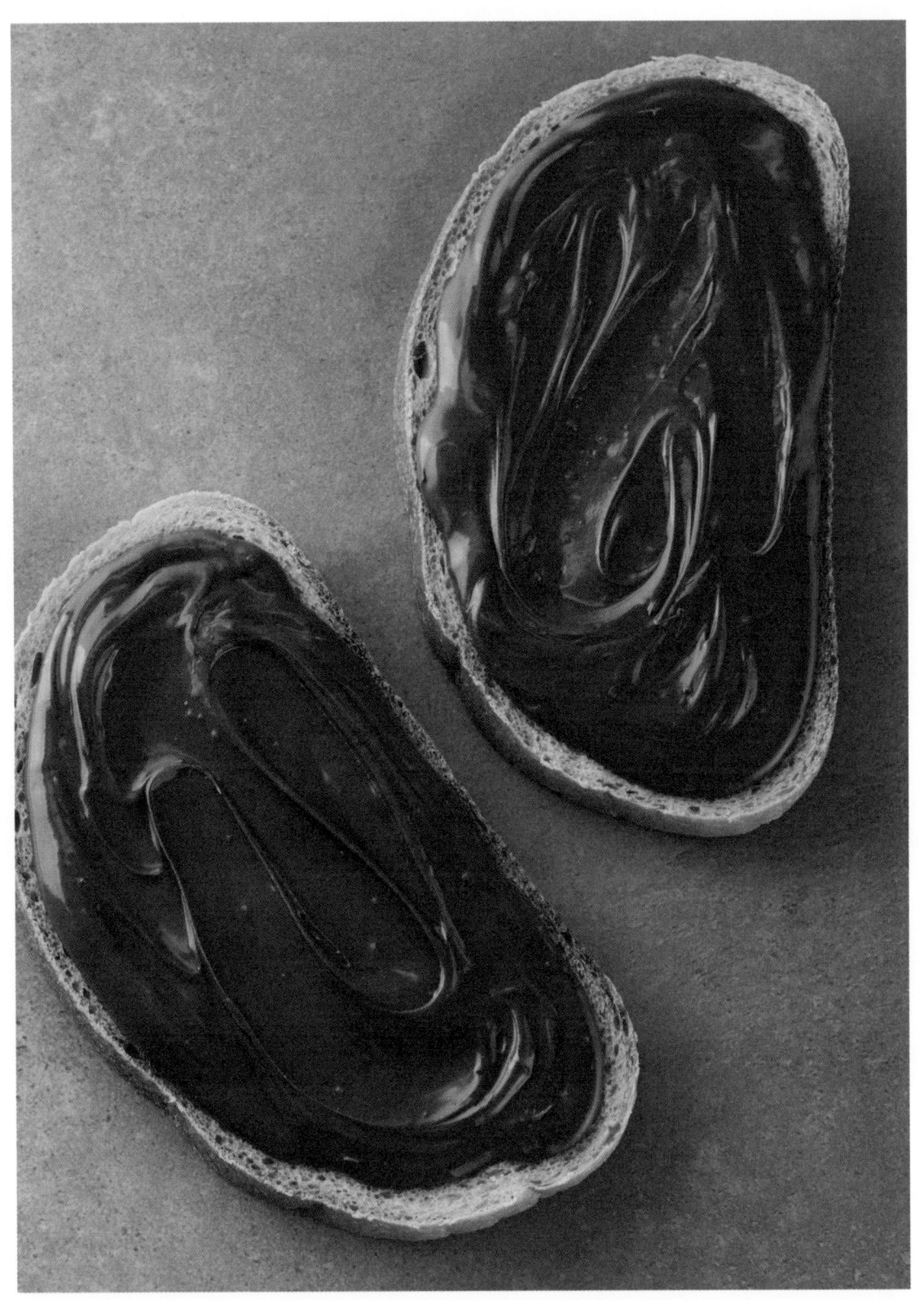

52 . THE FRENCH BAKERY COOKBOOK

TARTINE WITH MELTED CHOCOLATE AND CHOPPED NUTS

This is a staple snack for French children, but adults have trouble resisting it as well! The team at DPDI considers this childhood favorite one of the very best ways to enjoy bread. And the melted chocolate and nuts are superior to any store-bought spread. Replace hazelnuts with sliced almonds for a slight twist.

Large loaf or traditional baguette

Two bars of chocolate (dark or milk according to taste) per tartine

A few hazelnut kernels, ideally from Piedmont in Italy, which have previously been very roughly chopped with a knife or crushed by a rolling pin

Cream of balsamic vinegar, to taste

1. Cut one or more thick slices of bread or slice a baguette lengthwise.

2. Arrange the chocolate bars on the bread without overlapping.

3. Sprinkle on the hazelnuts.

4. Bake at 180°C/350°F for 5 to 7 minutes. Remove from oven.

5. Immediately pour a few drops of cream of balsamic vinegar on the tartines.

6. Wait courageously for the chocolate to cool, then let the magic go to work.

CHAPTER 2

LES VIENNOISERIES

Viennoiseries often goes hand in hand with a French bakery,
as it pertains to other products that are not bread (such
as brioche and croissants) but that are made through
a similar technique, or with nearly identical dough.

THE CROISSANT

When examining the display case at a French bakery and feasting on everything from sugar-dotted chouquettes to three-tiered, multicolored religieuses, it's easy to view golden-brown croissants as a bit plain. But there is nothing plain—or simple—about France's most beloved treat, including its origins.

The croissant was not born in France. Many attribute its origins to Vienna (where "viennoiserie" gets its name). But it goes back much further, according to some legends. Croissant is French for "crescent," the symbol of Islam. Some say that the earliest crescent-shaped cakes or breads were baked to celebrate Christian Europeans defeating Muslim forces, both at the Battle of Tours in 732 and in Vienna itself, where the Ottoman Empire was defeated in 1683. In the latter tale, bakers who were working through the night heard Ottoman forces digging tunnels under the city walls to begin their siege. The bakers sounded the alarm, the tunnels were destroyed, and the Ottomans were soundly beaten. The bakers then created baked goods in the shape of the crescent moon (which featured on their nemesis's flag) to celebrate.

Though some food historians disagree on how long crescent-shaped goods have been feasted upon, there's no denying that the modern-day croissant is the descendant of the Austrian kipferl. The kipferl, made of yeast-leavened dough, more closely resembles rugelach and can be served plain or filled with nuts. This variation was what was sold at Zang's pastry shop.

It was in 1915, however, that Sylvain Claudius Goy, a French pastry chef, recorded his recipe for the croissant made from laminated dough. Laminated dough, which results in flaky pastry, or pâte feuilletée, was a French technique dating back to the seventeenth century. At that time, it was never eaten on its own but was used to make a shell to hold meat or vegetable fillings, similar to a vol-au-vent. Marrying the kipferl and flaky pastry into one delicious snack confirmed what many have known for centuries: that the crust is the best part.

Flaky croissant is made from dough that has been layered with butter, then rolled and folded several times before being rolled out into a thin sheet. Though methods of incorporating butter can vary from baker to baker, the lamination process is crucial for achieving the soft and layered texture associated with croissants. This same dough is used for pain au chocolat (or chocolatines, depending on which region of France you find yourself in). Flaky pastry is used for other viennoiseries such as pain au raisin and chausson aux pommes.

LA BICYCLETTE

Williamsburg
667 Driggs Avenue
Brooklyn, NY 11211

Fort Greene
136 Dekalb Avenue
Brooklyn, NY 11217

Florent Andreytchenko, also known as Chef Flo, is one of those people who knew from a young age what he wanted to be when he grew up. While other kids might have named fireman or veterinarian as their future profession, Flo knew he was destined to become a baker.

"When I was six years old, my elementary school class went on a field trip to visit a bakery in my village. As soon as I walked in, I immediately knew this is what I wanted to do when I grew up," he explains. "The smell of freshly baked croissants, the heat of the kitchen, the baker's movements . . . In the afternoon, all the kids got a chance to make a very simple bread recipe, and that's it— I was hooked."

By the age of thirteen, he had already begun his first apprenticeship in his hometown in France's Champagne region. By eighteen, he was a full-time baker. Although he had fulfilled his childhood dream, there was still something missing: travel. He realized that he wanted to leave rural Champagne and see the world. His skill at making French bread was his ticket out.

At the age of twenty-one, he left for Australia, where he worked for Savico Basset Rouge at Brisbane's Le Bon Choix. Savico became his mentor and pushed him beyond his limits, inspiring him to then travel to New Zealand, Norway, Corsica, Croatia, Morocco, and Hong Kong, all while baking. After having lived in eight countries in eight years, he is now the proud owner of La Bicyclette, with two locations in Brooklyn. For *The French Bakery*, he proudly shares the recipe of one of France's most beloved treasures, the classic croissant.

LA BICYCLETTE'S CROISSANT

Yield: approx. 30 pieces

Although bagged, frozen, or fast-food versions exist, there is no replacement for a fresh and buttery croissant straight from a French bakery. The croissant has recently gained new followers in the form of donuts, cakes, and loaves, but the original crescent-shaped breakfast food is a timeless treat.

250 g Tradition or French-style flour (T65)

750 g gruau (high gluten) flour

300 g whole milk (4°C to 6°C/39°F to 43°F)

210 g water (4°C to 6°C/39°F to 43°F)

18 g salt

150 g granulated sugar

40 g baker's yeast

150 g cold unsalted butter

100 g levain

500 g sheet/lamination butter (cold from the refrigerator)

2 eggs

Pinch salt

1. Using a stand mixer, combine all ingredients, except sheet butter and eggs, in the bowl and mix at slow speed for approximately 10 minutes. Increase to second speed until smooth, approximately 6 minutes.

2. Remove the dough from the bowl, shape into a ball, wrap in plastic, and chill in the refrigerator for 24 hours.

3. Pound the sheet butter with a rolling pin until the butter starts to become malleable. Throughout the process, it's important for the butter to be just the right temperature—too cold and it will break, too warm and it will melt into the dough rather than layer on top of it.

4. Using a rolling pin, roll out the dough to ½-inch thickness in the form of a rectangle.

5. Place the sheet butter in the middle of the dough. It should fill the middle half. Fold the two sides over the top of the butter and use your fingers to press it closed.

6. Roll out the dough again to ½-inch thickness, keeping the rectangular form (with the long side facing you). From the right, measure 25% and fold the right side of the dough over to this mark. Fold the left side of the dough over to the same mark. Then fold the dough in half. Wrap in plastic and cool in the refrigerator for 30 minutes. It's important to work quickly during this step, to avoid the butter getting too warm.

7. Place the dough on your work surface with the short side toward you, open side facing right. Roll out (away from you) to

½-inch thickness. Turn the dough 90 degrees and fold in thirds. Wrap in plastic and cool in the refrigerator for 30 minutes.

8. Roll out the dough to ¼-inch thickness. You're aiming for a rectangle with dimensions approximately 25 inches by 22 inches, with the longer side facing you. Using a sharp knife, cut the dough in half lengthwise and put one piece precisely on top of the other.

9. Along the bottom of the dough rectangle, measure and mark every 3 inches. Along the top, measure and mark 1.5 inches once, then measure and mark every 3 inches. Using a sharp knife, make diagonal cuts to create triangles (you should have about 30 triangles, 15 from each layer of dough). Roll the triangles tightly, from the larger

end to the smaller end. If you don't want to make all of the croissants immediately, you can freeze the rolled croissants for up to one week. Defrost at room temperature before proofing.

10. Proof the croissants: Place on a baking tray lined with parchment paper. Leave at least 3 inches between each piece. Cover with a cotton or linen towel and let sit for 2.5 hours (ideal temperature is 25°C/77°F). The goal is for each piece to double in size.

11. Preheat the oven to 180°C/350°F.

12. Beat the eggs in a bowl, add a pinch of salt, and brush the egg wash on top of each piece.

13. Place in the oven and bake for 18 to 20 minutes.

CLASSIC KOUIGN-AMANN

Yield: 10 to 12 pieces

Classic Croissant
Dough (see below)

All-purpose flour for dusting

480 g sugar

Unsalted butter at room
temperature for the muffin tins

Classic Croissant Dough

522 g all-purpose flour, plus
more for dusting

75 g sugar

12 g fine sea salt

13 g unsalted butter, cut into
small pieces, softened
(about 18°C/65°F)

86 g cold water (7°C/45°F)

162 g poolish

50 g (6 tablespoons)
active dry yeast

113 g whole milk

16 g wildflower honey

Butter Block

308 g unsalted butter,
preferably high-fat European-
style (such as Plugra or
Beurremont), softened
(about 18°C/65°F)

Kouign-amann is a viennoiserie from Brittany. In the Breton language, still spoken in this western region of France, it translates to "butter cake." Over the past decade, kouign-amann has become fashionable and highly sought after in American French bakeries and is often filled with creams or ganaches for a sweeter variation. Pain D'Avignon's recipe returns to this treat's classic origins and calls for using a jumbo or Texas muffin tin and classic croissant dough.

CLASSIC CROISSANT DOUGH

1. In the bowl of a stand mixer fitted with the dough hook, combine the flour, sugar, and salt. Scatter the butter pieces over the dry ingredients. Set aside. In a separate bowl, combine the water, poolish, yeast, milk, and honey. Use your hands to dissolve the poolish in the liquid, squeezing it by the fistful until it is mostly dissolved. Pour the wet mixture into the flour mixture and mix the dough with your hands until it appears shaggy (the flour will not be entirely absorbed). Mix on low speed until the flour is completely absorbed. Increase the speed to medium-high and mix for about 3 minutes; it should be firm and smooth on the outside and reveal large holes in the center if you slice into it and pull it apart. (Take care not to overmix the dough.)

2. Remove the dough from the bowl and place on a clean work surface. Press the dough with your palms into a rough rectangle 1 inch thick, with a long side facing you. Pick up the dough and gently stretch it between your hands. Flip it over and turn it 90 degrees, so that a short side is now facing you. Push the top third of the dough away from you with the palm of your hand (this is the stretching), then roll the dough from the top onto itself toward you, using your thumbs to push firmly along the seam while resting your palms on top without pressing down on the dough. You should end up with a piece of log-shaped dough.

Continued...

Continue kneading this way until the dough is smooth and elastic, about 10 minutes. If the dough begins to stick to the work surface, dust it sparingly with flour. Shape the dough into a smooth ball and return it to the bowl. Press a piece of plastic wrap directly onto the surface of the dough and set aside to proof in a warm (24°C/75°F), draft-free spot until it doubles in volume, 1.5 to 2 hours, and passes the windowpane test. Gently punch the dough in the bowl to deflate it. Lightly dust a work surface with flour and turn the dough out onto it. Press into a 7-inch square. Wrap the dough in a double layer of plastic and refrigerate overnight.

3. Cut a 12x18-inch piece of parchment paper and lay it on a work surface. Fold it in half crosswise, then, using a ruler, measure 7 inches from the fold and crease the parchment parallel to the fold. Fold the right side of the rectangle at the 2-inch mark, then use the ruler to measure 7 inches across. Crease the parchment here, and fold along the left side. You should have a 7-inch square. Open up the parchment and put the butter in the center of the square. Fold the parchment along the creases to make a secure packet. Using a rolling pin, roll the butter out to the corners of the packet, making sure it forms an evenly thick square. Refrigerate until the butter is thoroughly chilled, 30 to 60 minutes. It should be firm, not malleable. Let it sit at room temperature for 5 to 10 minutes, until you can "fold" it without breaking it.

4. Fill a sheet pan with ice or ice packs and set it on a work surface to chill the surface before you set the dough on it. Transfer the dough from the refrigerator to the freezer for 15 to 20 minutes to firm it up; its temperature should register about 2°C/36°F. Test by pressing your thumb into it; it should leave an impression but require force to do so, and the dough should not bounce back. At the same time,

transfer the butter block to the countertop to sit for 5 to 10 minutes; the butter is the right consistency when it is slightly malleable and you can fold it in half without cracking or breaking it. If it is too soft, refrigerate it until it reaches that malleable consistency; if it is too hard, leave it out at room temperature until you can fold it without breaking it.

5. Remove the pan of ice from the work surface. Place the dough on the chilled surface, and with the palms of your hands, press it into a rectangle of even thickness, with a short side facing you. Position a rolling pin parallel to the edge of the work surface and roll out; begin in the middle and roll up, then return to the middle and roll down. Repeat rolling out the dough this way until it measures 14x7 inches. Cut the dough in half crosswise. Place the butter block on one of the halves, and then place the other half on top of the butter, aligning the edges. Lightly dust the work surface with flour. With a cut side of the dough packet parallel to the edge of the work surface, use the rolling pin to lightly tap out the dough, beginning in the middle and working to the top, then returning to the middle and tapping to the bottom. (The even tapping helps ensure that all the butter doesn't shift to one side of the dough.) Continue to roll and tap out the dough until it measures 21x7 inches; it should be a little less than ½-inch thick.

6. Brush any excess flour off the surface of the dough. Mark the dough evenly into three sections by measuring and marking the edge lightly with a sharp knife every 7 inches along a long side of the dough. Fold the dough into thirds at the imaginary lines: from the bottom third to the middle, followed by the top third to cover it, making sure the edges are aligned. (If there is a buckle, the butter won't laminate properly.) Turn the dough 90 degrees so that the folded edge is on either your left or

your right. Tap gently with the rolling pin as above and gently roll away from you to make a 10x7-inch rectangle. Wrap in plastic and freeze until the dough packet is firm, 20 to 30 minutes, checking periodically to make sure the butter doesn't get so cold that it becomes brittle (this can cause it to break through the layers and make it difficult to roll out).

7. Lightly dust a work surface with flour and place the dough packet on it, with a short side parallel to the edge of the work surface. Use the rolling pin to lightly tap out the dough, beginning in the middle and working to the top, then returning to the middle and tapping down. After tapping on the dough back and forth three times, flip the dough over and repeat the process, rolling out the dough until it measures 28x7 inches. As you roll it out, lift the dough gently with your hands to keep it from sticking to the work surface and to ensure that it's of even thickness. (Lightly dust the work surface with flour if the dough is sticking.) Brush any excess flour off the dough. Turn the dough 90 degrees so that a long side is parallel with the edge of the work surface. Eyeball an imaginary vertical line down the middle of the dough. Fold the dough, this time lifting the left side to the right, passing the imaginary centerline by about 1 inch. Then bring the right side to meet it; the meeting point will be off-center. Make sure to align the edges all the while. Keeping the meeting point off-center ensures that the gap between the two sides will stay closed while stretching.

KOUIGN-AMANN ASSEMBLY

1. Make the dough for the croissants through step 7 (the double fold), but do not cut the dough in half. Leave it whole.

2. Fill a sheet pan with ice or ice packs and set it on a work surface to chill the surface before you set the dough on it. Lightly dust

the surface with flour and place the dough on it with the fold to your left or right. With the rolling pin, gently tap the dough, working from the middle to the top and then from the middle to the bottom. Flip the dough over and continue to tap with the rolling pin until the dough is 7x21 inches and just shy of ½ inch thick. Brush any excess flour off the surface of the dough. Eyeball two horizontal lines to divide the dough into three equal sections. Fold the dough at the imaginary lines to make a 7x7-inch square, making sure the edges are aligned and flush; if there is a buckle, the butter won't laminate to the dough properly. Turn the dough 90 degrees so that a folded side is to your left (or right) again, tap gently with the rolling pin as above, and gently roll out to make a 7x10-inch rectangle. Wrap in plastic and freeze until the dough packet is firm, 20 to 30 minutes, checking periodically to make sure the butter doesn't get too cold and become brittle (this can cause it to break through the layers and make it difficult to roll out).

3. Repeat the single fold as above. After rolling the dough out to a 7x21-inch rectangle, eyeball two horizontal lines that divide the dough into three equal sections. Sprinkle 40 g of sugar evenly over the middle third of the dough. Fold the top third over the middle third (now halves), then sprinkle 40 more grams of sugar evenly on top of this fold. Fold the bottom half onto the middle to make a 7-inch square. Be sure that the edges are flush. Wrap tightly in plastic wrap and refrigerate for 1 hour. (Alternatively, freeze the dough overnight and transfer to the refrigerator 3 hours before using.) In both scenarios, when you press the dough between your two fingers, it should no longer be hard.

4. Fill a sheet pan with ice or ice packs and set it on a work surface to chill it. Dust the

Continued...

work surface lightly with flour, then place the dough on it, with the fold parallel to the edge. With the rolling pin at a 90-degree angle to the edge of your work surface, roll the dough out to a rectangle ⅛ inch thick and about 10x18 inches, working from the middle to the right and then from the middle to the left. If the dough resists stretching, wrap it up and return it to the refrigerator until firm. Lift the dough as you work to prevent it from sticking to the surface and to gauge its overall thickness; you want it to be even. With a long side parallel to the edge, press your index finger along the top of the dough to anchor it to the work surface. Sprinkle 100 g of sugar evenly over the dough, leaving a 1-inch border along the top edge (this bare border will help the dough seal properly). Roll up the dough like a carpet, beginning on one end and tucking it tightly as you work across to the other end and taking care not to pull or stretch the dough. Place the rolled dough seam-side down on the work surface. Trim the ends (you can use them to add to other pieces as necessary to make them all even).

With a sharp knife, slice the roll crosswise into 1½- to 1¾-inch-thick rounds to yield 10 to 12 rounds. Pour 200 g of the sugar into a shallow bowl. Lightly rub 10 or 12 cups of a Texas muffin tin with the softened butter. Dredge each round of dough in the sugar, turning it over and onto its sides to coat completely. Place a round in each buttered cup, then press down gently so that the bottom sits flat.

5. Cover the muffin tin with an overturned plastic bin and let the pastries proof in a warm (24°C/75°F), draft-free spot until the cups are three-quarters full, 30 to 45 minutes. (The empty spaces on the bottom of the cup will be filled in and the dough will come to within ⅛ inch of the sides of it.)

6. Position a rack in the center of the oven and preheat the oven to 215°C/420°F. Sprinkle the kouign-amann with the remaining 100 g of sugar, dividing evenly. Slide the muffin tin onto a baking sheet. Bake until the pastries are deep golden and the sugar is caramelized, 25 to 30 minutes, rotating the pan front to back halfway through.

BRIOCHE

On your journey from tasting traditional savory loaves of bread to sweet and layered viennoiserie, you'll encounter brioche—and likely never want to leave. Brioche is a type of French bread that could easily disguise itself as something far more rich. It's both simple and sophisticated. Although divine enough on its own, chefs across the globe can't resist stuffing it with fruit, piling it high with everything from butter to caviar, or soaking it in eggs and frying it up as the ultimate French toast.

Part of what makes brioche so delicious is the high volume of egg and butter used to make it (part of what gives its crumb a soft texture and golden color). Like other viennoiseries, brioche is made in the same way as bread but is considered more luxurious because of added eggs, butter, liquids, or even sugar. And, true to its form, it is enjoyed at breakfast but also as an afternoon snack. In fine dining restaurants across the United States, brioche has replaced the dinner roll as a more upscale bread option.

This association with luxury is nothing new. Starting with Louis XIV, brioche has long been considered a bread product fit for a king. This is due to the high quantity of butter in a brioche recipe—butter that French peasants could not afford. The famous expression, "Let them eat cake," was actually "Qu'ils mangent de la brioche," or let them eat brioche. (This phrase was not uttered by Marie Antoinette but rather an anonymous princess—and overheard by the revolutionary writer Jean-Jacques Rousseau.)

Similar to but not to be confused with brioche are pain au lait and gâche, which are made from similar dough with added milk. Most regions in France have variations of brioche that can be braided, covered with sugar, or contain hidden treats such as pralines, chocolate chips, or fruit.

MIOLIN BAKERY

Claudio Miolin's professional career as both a trained culinary chef and professional baker has spanned over fifteen years and three continents. Having worked in top kitchens in Berlin, Sydney, Stockholm, and New York, Claudio brings a unique perspective and experience to everything he creates. Specializing in artisanal baking with the highest quality ingredients, Claudio founded Miolin Bakery in 2020, based out of Brooklyn, New York.

MIOLIN'S BRIOCHE

Less like bread and more like a buttery cloud, brioche has always been one of the most decadent carriers for everything from strawberry jam to cream and caviar. Claudio Miolin's recipe can be used for multiple purposes, but transforming it into berry-covered French toast is probably the best place to start.

191 g all-purpose flour, plus more for dusting

29 g granulated sugar

4 g fine sea salt

3 g instant dry yeast

94 g unsalted butter, chilled

74 g whole eggs, whisked

37 g egg yolk

18 g whole milk

Egg Wash

50 g whole eggs, whisked

10 g whole milk

1. Whisk together flour, sugar, salt, and instant dry yeast in a mixing bowl.

2. Cut butter into 10 cubes and place the cubes in the refrigerator.

3. Add eggs and milk to the flour mixture in a stand mixer fitted with the dough hook attachment and mix the dough at medium speed for about 10 minutes. Scrape the bowl, if necessary, in the mixing process.

4. Once the dough has developed some strength and elasticity, add one piece of butter at a time while mixing on medium speed until it's fully incorporated into the dough before adding the next piece. This should take another 8 to 10 minutes at medium speed. It should form a soft and smooth ball and should be slightly shiny.

5. Pour dough onto a slightly floured countertop and form the dough into a ball.

6. Place the dough in a bowl pre-greased with cooking spray and cover with plastic wrap. Let rest for 30 minutes at room temperature.

7. Refrigerate the dough for at least 7 hours. This will slow down the fermentation process and chill the butter, which makes the dough easier to shape.

8. Place your dough on a lightly floured countertop and press the dough with your hand into a rectangle, then roll the dough into a log and place the log seam side down into a loaf pan (8.5x4.5x2.75) pre-greased with cooking spray.

9. Lightly cover the loaf pan with a piece of pre-greased plastic wrap and let it sit at room temperature until the dough has risen to reach the rim of the pan, about 2 to 3 hours.

10. Preheat the oven to 190°C/375°F.

11. To create the egg wash, combine eggs and milk in a mixing bowl until well mixed.

12. Brush the brioche with the egg wash and bake in a preheated oven on the middle rack for 30 to 35 minutes. After 20 minutes, create a tent over the brioche with tin foil to bake fully without getting too dark.

13. Let the brioche sit in the loaf pan for 10 minutes before transferring onto a wire rack.

CRÊPES

This French classic, which is as easy to make at home as it is to order out, is more appropriate for snack time, dessert, or even dinner than it is for breakfast, unlike its American cousin the pancake. Paper-thin and light as air, crêpes are best served hot, sprinkled with sugar and lemon juice, drizzled with honey and orange blossom essence, or smeared with Nutella.

250 g heavy cream

250 g milk

100 g butter, melted

200 g all-purpose flour

150 g granulated sugar

6 g fine sea salt

300 g whole eggs, whisked

1. Temper the cream and milk in a saucepan to 85°C/185°F.

2. Once at desired temperature, remove from heat and add the melted butter. Stir.

3. In a separate bowl, whisk together flour, sugar, and salt.

4. Once the milk and cream mixture cools, add whisked eggs. Mix until combined.

5. Pour the liquid mixture over the dry ingredients and whisk until smooth.

6. Cover with plastic wrap and set overnight in the refrigerator.

7. Remove bowl from the refrigerator 30 minutes prior to cooking and let batter come to room temperature.

8. Heat a nonstick pan (8-inch to 10-inch) over medium heat and spray with a cooking spray or a small amount of butter.

9. Scoop one ladle of batter onto the pan and swirl pan to make sure the batter completely and evenly covers the pan.

10. Once the top of the crêpe turns from liquid to dry, flip it and cook for an additional 30 seconds.

11. Pair with Nutella, cinnamon sugar, or desired jam. For more savory crêpes, decrease sugar by 50 g.

AYA BAKERY

1332 W Grand Avenue
Chicago, IL 60642

Located in West Town Chicago, Aya Pastry celebrates the best of seasonal ingredients, with products crafted with precision and love by pastry chef Aya Fukai. Aya Pastry offers a creative take on signature breads along with celebratory cakes, whimsical sweets, and breakfast pastries.

Aya won Eater's National Pastry Chef of the Year in 2016, was nominated in 2017 for James Beard Outstanding Pastry Chef, and won the Chicago Tribune's Pastry Chef of the Year in 2018. The bakery recently received the "Best New Baked Good Empire" title for the 2021 Eater Awards.

BRIOCHE À LA CANNELLE

Yield: 6 pieces

A flavor profile often associated with American breakfast, Aya's cinnamon buns start with a brioche-inspired yeasted dough. The addition of sticky pecan frosting is traditional in North America—and all the rage in Europe.

Cinnamon Roll Dough

240 g whole milk

14 g (2 packets) yeast

67 g granulated sugar

2 extra large eggs

560 g bread flour

10 g salt

114 g butter, softened and divided

Cinnamon Sugar

100 g (½ cup) granulated sugar

5 g (2 teaspoon) ground cinnamon

1. To begin making the dough, whisk together milk, yeast, sugar, and eggs in a stand mixer bowl.

2. Place the flour, salt, and ¾ stick butter on top of the mixture. (Reserve ¼ stick butter for later use.)

3. Combine ingredients in the mixer with a dough hook and mix on medium speed for 5 minutes.

4. Let dough rest in the bowl in a warm room until it has doubled in size.

5. Punch down the dough and place in the refrigerator.

6. Preheat the oven to 165°C/325°F.

7. Combine the ingredients in the cinnamon sugar recipe and set aside.

8. After the dough has rested in the refrigerator for at least 2 hours, roll the dough out to a 10x14-inch rectangle.

9. Melt the remaining ¼ stick butter. With a pastry brush, lightly brush the bottom and the sides of an ovenproof baking dish. Sprinkle just enough of the cinnamon sugar mix to stick to the buttered pan. Use the rest of the butter to brush the top of the rolled-out dough with melted butter.

10. Sprinkle the remaining cinnamon sugar mixture on top of the buttered dough and press it into the dough lightly to make it stick.

11. Roll the dough into a log shape and cut it into 6 equal pieces using a sharp knife.

12. Place the buns an equal distance apart with the swirl side up.

13. Cover the buns lightly with plastic wrap and let them double in size in a warm room or proof in a Monogram oven using the proofing setting.

14. Bake for 20 minutes, turn the tray, and bake for another 5 to 10 minutes. (Adjust according to different household ovens, until a knife inserted in the middle comes out clean.)

STICKY PECAN FROSTING

280 g light brown sugar

140 g butter

5 g salt

500 g condensed milk

180 g toasted pecan pieces

1. In a small saucepan, melt together light brown sugar and butter over medium heat.

2. Add salt and condensed milk and cook while stirring with a spatula until bubbling and thick.

3. Add the toasted pecans and stir.

4. Top the cinnamon rolls while the frosting is warm.

JACOB FRAIJO
AND CHRISTINA HANKS

Jacob Fraijo and Christina Hanks met in 2011 and have worked side by side in French-inspired patisseries, bakeries, and restaurants ever since. In Los Angeles, San Francisco, New York City, and Paris, they have honed their skills and love of bread and pastry. Their talents have led them to lead roles in pastry kitchens for Michelin-star chefs such as Dominique Crenn and Thomas Keller.

In 2020 the couple settled in their hometown in Southern California, where the concept of their own cottage bakery was born. Pavé Bakery was the culmination of each of their focuses: Jacob's expertise in bread and Christina's mastery of patisserie. They pay respect to the tradition and technique of French baking but apply it to their setting in California. For them, that means sourcing local ingredients as an effort to live and operate sustainably. This involves directly sourcing produce from local farmers, buying raw honey from beekeepers, and purchasing California chocolate and fresh heirloom whole grain flours from millers to give guests the most flavorful, nutritional, and fresh pastry, bread, and cakes possible. Jacob and Christina focus on quality and simplicity with their menu offerings so that these special ingredients can shine through.

For *The French Bakery*, the duo has contributed two spins on iconic French bakes: brioche and canelé. Ideal sweet treats for almost any time of the day, these two recipes start with the basics but show home bakers and pastry chefs how to build off these recipes and add their own personal touch.

TARTE BRIOCHÉE AUX FRAISES

This combination of fluffy brioche and dessert-like fillings is sure to wow at any dinner party or spring gathering, making it worth the effort of a two-day preparation. Prepare yourself for success by making the almond cream and brioche dough 24 hours in advance and then finalizing the dessert the next day.

Almond Cream

Yield: 314 g

75 g butter, softened

75 g powdered sugar, sifted

75 g almond meal

9 g all-purpose flour

75 g eggs, room temperature

2 g dark rum

5 g vanilla extract

ALMOND CREAM

1. In a stand mixer with a paddle attachment or in a small bowl with a rubber spatula, paddle the butter until smooth.

2. Gradually add in the powdered sugar and mix just until smooth, not aerated.

3. Add in the rest of the dry ingredients gradually. Mix and scrape down the bowl so the mixture homogenizes between each addition.

4. Add the egg, rum, and vanilla extract and mix well.

5. Store in the refrigerator for up to 5 days.

Brioche Dough

Yield: 780 g 3 strawberry almond brioche tarts or 1 loaf of brioche

101 g whole milk

60 g eggs

60 g egg yolks

195 g all-purpose flour

84 g high gluten flour

28 g granulated sugar

3 g milk powder

4 g dry instant yeast

6 g sea salt

168 g butter, unsalted

1 quart ripe strawberries

BRIOCHE DOUGH

Day 1 Mixing:

1. Weigh out all ingredients and chill them completely in the refrigerator before mixing.

2. In a stand mixer with a hook attachment, combine the milk, eggs, egg yolks, both flours, sugar, milk powder, yeast, and salt. Liquids should go into the bowl first, then dry ingredients on top. Reserve the cold butter.

3. Using a rolling pin or dowel, pound the butter until it is pliable, and set aside until the first stage of mixing is complete.

4. Mix on low speed for 3 minutes. Mix on medium speed for 3 minutes.

Continued...

5. Scrape down the mixing bowl and keep the mixer on medium speed.

6. In 3 parts, add the cold but pliable butter to the mixer, making sure each incorporation is mostly combined before adding the next.

7. Once all the butter is incorporated, continue mixing until dough has gained full development and pulls a smooth and glossy window. This usually happens in 6 to 7 minutes after the butter is incorporated but may vary. The dough should also begin mounding on the hook at this point. The temperature of the dough should not exceed 24°C/75°F.

8. Once the dough is finished mixing, remove it from the mixer and form an even mass.

9. Flatten the dough onto a tray lined with plastic film. Completely wrap the dough in film.

10. Chill the dough quickly in the freezer. After about an hour, when the dough increases in size, unwrap the film and punch the dough down. Rewrap.

11. Leave the brioche in the refrigerator overnight until ready to divide.

Day 2 Finishing and Baking:

1. On a floured surface, divide 260 g portions and ball into rounds. Let dough rest for about 20 minutes, covered.

2. Using a small amount of flour and a rolling pin or dowel, evenly roll out the round so that it is about 6 inches in diameter.

3. Place the brioche rounds onto a parchment- or Silpat-lined tray, allowing enough space for the brioche to expand to about 8 to 9 inches after baking.

4. Place plastic wrap loosely over the trays and proof at 26°C to 27°F/78°F to 80°F about 1.5 to 2 hours. Spray water on the dough as needed to prevent a skin from developing.

5. While the brioche is proofing, bring the almond cream to room temperature and prepare the strawberries. Wash, pat dry, and hull the strawberries.

6. Once the brioche is proofed, press small pieces of cold cubed butter (about 5 g each) into the rounds, allowing space for the dough to come up between each one. Place a strawberry on each piece of butter. Sprinkle a small amount of sugar onto each strawberry.

7. Pipe almond cream around each strawberry and generously top the brioche with raw, sliced almonds.

8. Bake at 182°C/360°F for 12 minutes, rotate the tray, and bake for another 8 to 12 minutes.

9. Check for even golden color on top and bottom of the brioche. Almond cream on top of brioche should spring back and not appear wet.

10. Dust with powdered sugar and enjoy warm.

BRIOCHE LOAF

Double the brioche dough recipe to yield enough dough to make 1 loaf and 3 strawberry almond brioche, or 2 brioche loaves. Or make just 1 recipe for 1 loaf.

1. For one 10x5-inch loaf pan, use about 700 g of dough.

2. On a lightly floured surface, shape the loaf by flattening the portion of dough into a rectangle. Roll the portion of dough up to make a log about the length of the loaf pan. Place the dough inside the loaf pan, seam side down.

3. Proof in the same fashion as above.

4. Bake at 360°F for about 45 to 60 minutes. The internal temperature of the cooked brioche should be 94°C/201°F.

5. Unmold loaf immediately on a cooling rack.

LES GAUFRES

Yield: 8 waffles

"The creation of the perfect waffle is in the crispiness of the outer crust and the mellowness of the inside. It will take a few trials before you get the perfect waffle. Some waffle irons differ from others. Never add sugar to the recipe. This will ruin your waffle iron and leave you with a hell of a chore to clean it of all the burnt and caramelized sugar. The sweetness in the waffle comes from the sprinkled powdered sugar and the few grams of sugar in the whipped cream."

—Chef Renaud Hendrickx

5 egg yolks

8 egg whites, beaten

200 g flour

2 pinches salt

150 g melted butter

375 g warm milk

Powdered sugar, for topping

Whipping cream, for topping

1. Turn on the waffle iron to 220°C/425°F.

2. Separate egg yolks from whites.

3. Beat the whites to firm with a pinch of salt.

4. Pour the flour into a large bowl.

5. Add one pinch of salt.

6. Make a volcano and add the yolks.

7. Add the melted butter and the warm milk and whisk to obtain a smooth batter. Then add the egg whites, delicately.

8. Pour a ladle of batter on one side of your double waffle iron to fill all the alveolar. Close the empty side of the iron onto the batter side and immediately turn the waffle iron to the opposite side. This will allow the batter to bake on both surfaces (10 minutes).

9. Once the batter has baked, it will be easy to open your waffle iron. Use a two-pronged waffle fork to poke through the waffle lengthwise to extract it and then the other.

10. Place your hot waffles on a serving plate, sprinkle with powdered sugar, and place four dollops of whipped cream unevenly.

THE FRENCH BASTARDS

61, rue Oberkampf
Paris, France 75011

181, rue Saint-Denis
Paris, France 75002

35 place Saint-Ferdinand
Paris, France 75017

The name of this bakery is supposed to get your attention. Although "French bastard" refers to what cofounder Julien Abourmad was lovingly called by his Australian coworkers at a Down Under establishment he once worked for, there's more to it than just that. Bâtard is actually a type of traditional French bread. By translating it into English, Julien and his cofounders, David Abehsera and Emmanuel Gunther, have signaled that their bakery is a fully modern twist on the traditional.

The three artisans and best friends are considered leaders among a new generation of bakers and pastry chefs, with storefronts now present in the Oberkampf, Saint-Denis, and Place Saint Ferdinand neighborhoods of Paris. These locations are far from the bourgeois and residential 15th arrondissement where the trio grew up, and are located in the decidedly more hip, young, and, yes, hipster eastern Paris.

Lines to each location spill out the door and wrap around the corner. What are fans coming for? New offerings that are a mix of French, European, and Anglo-Saxon influences: iced banana bread, beignets stuffed with homemade hazelnut spread, and other rich, sweet, and made-for-Instagram bites. For 2022, they introduced a "pain des rois" collaboration with pastry chef François Daubinet that was a spinoff of the traditional galette des rois served for Epiphany in January. The outside resembled a rye loaf while the inside was filled with rich frangipane. Their Epiphany bake for 2023 was a cruffin des rois, the cruffin (cousin to the cronut) being one of their signature goods.

Although known for attention-grabbing bakes, they also offer hearty and wholesome breads, such as seeded or rye loaves. But the Bastards aren't looking to be put on the map for their wholesomeness. Their recipes for *The French Bakery* include a caramel-filled kouglof and two variations of beignets that are anything but innocent.

CARAMEL PRALINE KOUGLOF

Yield: 6 pieces

A kouglof is a traditional recipe from the Alsace region in France made from yeast-risen enriched dough. Similar in shape to a Bundt cake, the kouglof is often filled with nuts or raisins. The French Bastards' version is a more decadent take on the classic recipe, calling for almond praline and extra caramel.

Almond Praline

37 g almonds

25 g granulated sugar

9 g water

Kouglof Dough

236 g pastry flour

142 g eggs

50 g granulated sugar

5 g salt

9 g milk

7 g yeast

118 g butter

71 g almond praline (see above)

24 g Sosa caramel crispy

1. Make the almond praline: Roast the almonds for a few minutes in the oven at 180°C/350°F. In a saucepan, heat the sugar and water. Then add the roasted almonds. Mix with a spatula so that the almonds can caramelize. Pour them into a container and let them cool before blending to obtain small praline pieces.

2. For the kouglof dough, mix the flour, eggs, sugar, salt, milk, and yeast in a mixer with a hook attachment. When the dough no longer sticks to the sides of the bowl, add butter and mix again. When the dough is no longer sticking to the sides of the bowl yet again, mix in the praline and caramel crispy. Let the dough rest in the refrigerator for 1.5 hours.

3. Roll the dough into 110 g balls and slightly hollow out the center so that the piece of dough will fit into a Bundt cake mold. Let the dough rise somewhere that's 28°C/82°F. (In the winter, use your turned-off oven in which you have placed a container of hot water ahead of time.)

4. Heat oven to 165°C/325°F and bake for 15 to 18 minutes.

NOTE: Fill the hollow area of your kouglof with liquid caramel before serving.

HAZELNUT SPREAD BEIGNETS

Yield: 6 pieces

The beignet is a donut with a French accent. The French Bastards' variation is distinctively European with its addition of homemade hazelnut spread, a nod to the Nutella that features in so many childhood—and let's face it, adult—sweet treats.

Beignet Dough

27 g beer

79 g heavy cream

79 g eggs

238 g flour

40 g granulated sugar

5 g brown sugar

3 g salt

11 g yeast

Frying oil, as needed

Sugar, for dusting

Hazelnut Praline

24 g hazelnuts

7 g water

22 g granulated sugar

Hazelnut Spread

29 g hazelnuts

42 g dark gianduja (chocolate-hazelnut mixture)

42 g milk gianduja

39 g hazelnut praline (see above)

6 g butter

12 g powdered milk

6 g cocoa powder

1. Prepare the beignet dough: In a mixer, combine the beer, cream, and eggs, then add the flour, sugar, brown sugar, salt, and yeast. Start the mixer; when the dough no longer sticks to the sides, stop and take the temperature of the mixture. It should be between 23°C and 24°C/73°F and 75°F. When this temperature is reached, keep the dough in a container in the refrigerator for 3 hours.

2. Divide the dough into 6 pieces, about 80 g each, and place them on a tray to rest in the refrigerator for another 30 minutes.

3. Pull them out and let them rest for another 2 hours at room temperature.

4. Heat the frying oil to 160°C/320°F in a fryer or a deep pan. Fry each beignet for 5 to 8 minutes on each side.

5. When the beignets are golden brown, set them on absorbent paper towels, then roll them in sugar.

6. For the praline: Roast the hazelnuts for a few minutes in the oven at 180°C/350°F. Let them cool. Prepare a light caramel by heating the water and sugar. Blend the roasted hazelnuts together with the caramel until the entire preparation is liquid.

7. For the hazelnut spread, heat a dry pan and roast the hazelnuts for a few minutes. Let them cool, then blend them until you have a paste.

8. In a saucepan, melt the 2 gianduja. Add the hazelnut paste and the praline. Mix together well. Melt the butter before adding it to the mix, and then add the powdered milk and the cocoa powder. Mix well so that all the ingredients are fully incorporated.

9. Fill the beignets with the hazelnut spread, 30 g per beignet, before eating!

NOTE: You can add a little bit of neutral-flavored oil to the praline if it isn't liquid enough.

VANILLA AND HAZELNUT PRALINE BEIGNETS

Yield: 6 pieces

This variation of the beignet recipe calls for delicate, vanilla-flavored crème pâtissière. Don't mistake delicate for light, however. Although not as rich as chocolate and hazelnut, this twist is still decidedly decadent.

Beignet Dough

27 g beer

79 g heavy cream

79 g eggs

238 g flour

40 g granulated sugar

5 g brown sugar

3 g salt

11 g yeast

Frying oil, as needed

Sugar, for dusting

Crème Pâtissière

122 g milk

10 g cream powder

24 g granulated sugar

24 g egg yolks

1 vanilla bean

Praline

69 g hazelnuts

16 g water

46 g granulated sugar

20 g milk

1. Prepare the beignet dough: In a mixer, combine the beer, cream, and eggs, then add the flour, sugar, brown sugar, salt, and yeast. Start the mixer; when the dough no longer sticks to the sides, stop and take the temperature of the mixture. It should be between 23°C and 24°C/73°F and 75°F. When this temperature is reached, keep the dough in a container in the refrigerator for 3 hours.

2. Divide the dough into 6 pieces, about 80 g each, and place them on a tray to rest in the refrigerator for another 30 minutes.

3. Pull them out and let them rest for another 2 hours at room temperature.

4. Heat the frying oil to 160°C/320°F in a fryer or a deep pan. Fry each beignet for 5 to 8 minutes on each side.

5. When the beignets are golden brown, set them on absorbent paper towels, then roll them in sugar.

6. Prepare the crème pâtissière: Simmer the milk in a saucepan. Mix the cream powder and sugar together in a bowl. Add the egg yolks to the dry ingredients and whisk together. Add half of the milk and whisk again. Then add the entire mixture to the rest of the milk in the saucepan as well as the scraped insides of the vanilla bean. Bring everything to a boil and let boil for 35 seconds, mixing without stopping so that the cream does not burn. Let the mixture cool before storing it in the refrigerator.

7. For the praline: Roast the hazelnuts for a few minutes in an oven at 180°C/350°F. Let them cool. Prepare a light caramel by heating the water and sugar. Blend the roasted hazelnuts together with the caramel until the entire preparation is liquid. Add the milk to the praline at the very end.

8. Fill the beignets with the crème pâtissière (30 g per beignet) and praline (25 g per beignet) before eating.

NOTE: You can add a little bit of neutral-flavored oil to the praline if it isn't liquid enough.

CHAPTER 3

LA PÂTISSERIE

A French pastry chef can technically be responsible for everything that is not bread and viennoiserie, whether that be rustic tarts or towering chocolate sculptures. These offerings are often, but not exclusively, associated with dessert. In this chapter, we'll focus on recipes that primarily have to do with the five master doughs: puff pastry, choux pastry, shortcrust pastry, pie dough, and phyllo dough.

PÂTE FEUILLETÉE: FLAKY OR PUFF PASTRY

Flaky or puff pastry relies on heavy amounts of butter to obtain its rich and delicious bite. The name originates from *feuille*, which translates to both "leaf" and "sheet of paper," underlining its layered look. The layers are achieved through the lamination process, where butter and dough are folded together multiple times before baking.

Pâte feuilletée is a staple for most pastry chefs, but the lamination process is known for being maddeningly time-consuming. Made from flour, butter, water, and salt, it can be used for both savory and sweet dishes, from hors d'oeuvres to millefeuilles.

PÂTE À CHOUX: CHOUX PASTRY

Choux pastry, or *pâte à choux*, is often associated with the most decadent of treats, like cream-filled éclairs, colorful religieuses, and towering croquembouche. But its name stems from a more wholesome origin. In French, *chou* means "cabbage." The airy concoctions made from choux pastry are meant to resemble small heads of cabbage.

Although their layers are somewhat similar to those found in flaky puff pastry, choux pastry technique is entirely different. This hybrid of dough and batter is actually cooked twice. Strangely enough, it starts in a saucepan, where flour, milk or water, and butter are combined together over heat. Eggs are added once the mixture is removed from heat, and then the dough is either piped or spooned out into its intended shape.

Once baked, it becomes delicately crisp on the outside and hollow on the inside, making it ideal for cream or jam fillings. It's not uncommon to find pearl sugar, crumbly *craquelin*, or icing on top of choux, as well. As with most French baking and pastry, both savory and sweet variations of choux exist. One can enjoy a simple, sugar-dusted *chouquette* with afternoon tea or a Gruyère-filled *gougère* with a glass of wine or kir before dinner.

PÂTE SABLÉE: SHORTCRUST PASTRY

Shortcrust pastry, or *pâte sablée*, is known for its melt-in-your-mouth, buttery, dense bite as well as its "sandy" texture that gives sablé its name. To achieve shortcrust pastry, the butter is added directly to all dry ingredients, then mixed together to achieve a sand-like texture.

Pâte sablée is often associated with cookies, particularly *sablés Bretons*, which are decadent two-bite cookies made from Brittany butter. The dough can also be the perfect base for certain pies and tarts. Because of its density, it's preferred for creamy, liquid-based, sure-to-stain fillings—think chocolate silk, lemon cream, or blueberry.

PÂTE BRISÉE: PIE DOUGH

*L*a *pâte brisée* is the French version of pie dough. Literally translating to "broken dough," the ingredients in French pie dough are similar to shortcrust pastry but are made in a way to eliminate the latter's well-known sandy texture. Compared to American pie dough, pâte brisée has a higher ratio of butter to flour. It is considered the ideal dough for savory bakes such as quiches.

Somewhere between shortcrust and pie dough is *pâte sucrée*, another popular pie dough that is lightly sweet. Butter and sugar are creamed together before mixing with other ingredients, making it less crumbly than shortcrust but sweeter than traditional pâte brisée. Consider this the ultimate dough for fruit-filled pies.

PÂTÉ SUCRÉE

Yield: 2 (9-Inch) Crusts

If you want a sweet piecrust, this is your best bet. It also makes a wonderful tart shell.

8 oz. unsalted butter, softened

8 oz. sugar

¼ teaspoon kosher salt

1 egg

2 egg yolks

1 lb. all-purpose flour, plus more as needed

1. In the work bowl of a stand mixer fitted with the paddle attachment, cream the butter, sugar, and salt on medium until the mixture is creamy, light, and fluffy, about 5 minutes.

2. Add the egg and egg yolks and beat until incorporated. Add the flour and beat until the mixture comes together as a dough.

3. Place the dough on a flour-dusted work surface and fold it over itself until it is a ball. Divide the dough in two and flatten each piece into a 1-inch-thick disc. Cover each piece completely with plastic wrap and place the dough in the refrigerator for at least 2 hours before rolling it out to fit your pie plate.

PÂTE PHYLLO: PHYLLO PASTRY

Phyllo pastry or phyllo dough can be found in both savory and sweet recipes all over France, but it is more closely associated with Middle Eastern or Balkan origins. Phyllo, also named filo, comes from the Greek word for "leaf" and refers to the thin layers this particular dough is known for. The pastry dough is unleavened and rolled paper-thin. It is brushed with oil or butter before being baked.

Greeks, Turks, and Armenians argue over who actually invented phyllo pastry. In Greek epics such as Homer's *Odyssey*, there is the first reference to thinly rolled "bread" filled with honey and nuts. In Turkish records, there are also mentions of desserts made from "folded" bread. In France and in pastry shops the world over, the end results are treats such as baklava, filled with various nuts, honey, and dried fruits.

Although not technically French, the importance of understanding phyllo is essential to any formally trained pastry chef. The French have incorporated this "master" dough into many dishes, particularly *briques* and feuilletés, which are savory phyllo-based recipes filled with cheese or cooked vegetables, similar to the Greek spanakopita.

ALICE JAROSZUK

Alice Jaroszuk is a pastry chef who was born and raised in Poland, but she developed her high-level skills across Europe and the United States. Alice began her career with a degree in culinary arts from the Institut Paul Bocuse in France. She went on to work in some of Europe's most illustrious Michelin-star kitchens, including Emmanuel Renaut's Flocons de Sel in Megève, France; Rasmus Kofoed's Geranium in Copenhagen; Air du Temps, Pierre Marcolini, and Khobz in Belgium; and Atelier Crenn in the United States.

Through her work and travels, she gained a network of trusted culinary colleagues who have invited her on to develop pastry and desserts. One such example includes Maligne in Seaside, California. The millefeuille recipe, a classic French pastry to which Alice gave a California twist with the addition of fresh figs, hails from Maligne's dessert menu.

Back in Europe, Chef Alice is now developing a project, Goods, alongside two colleagues. Goods is a bakery in the heart of Brussels, Belgium, that focuses on bread, viennoiseries, and fermentation, as well as light fare and music. Goods uses seasonal products only and adds twists to classics while also respecting ingredients in their simplicity. The smoky, miso-based spin on the classic chocolate tart that Alice has contributed to *The French Bakery* comes to us from Goods.

MILLEFEUILLE AUX FIGUES

A millefeuille is an iconic French pastry named for its thousands of layers, or "leaves," of pastry. Beyond puff pastry and cream, a millefeuille can be flavored with vanilla, chocolate, or any number of fruit flavorings. Here, pastry chef Alice Jaroszuk adds figs in two different layers: a fig-leaf infused crème diplomate and fresh figs added when plating.

Puff Pastry

1 sheet puff pastry

50 g granulated sugar

50 g butter

6 or 7 medium-sized figs per portion

Fig Leaf Crème Diplomate

9 g gelatin sheets

500 g milk, infused with fig leaves (can also be replaced by vanilla beans)

35 g vanilla sugar

6 egg yolks

35 g vanilla sugar

27 g cornstarch

40 g butter, chilled

250 g whipped cream

PUFF PASTRY

1. Preheat the oven to 190°C/375°F.

2. Cut the puff pastry into 7 cm circles.

3. Prepare your baking sheets: brush 2 sheets of parchment paper with butter on one side and sprinkle with sugar.

4. Place the discs of dough on one of the prepared baking sheets. Place the second sheet of parchment on top, then a sheet pan for weight.

5. Bake in the oven for 15 minutes, until golden brown and caramelized on both sides.

FIG LEAF CRÈME DIPLOMATE

1. Rehydrate gelatin sheets in ice cold water.

2. Pour the milk into a saucepan.

3. Add 35 g of sugar, place over medium-high heat, and bring to just under a boil, stirring occasionally.

4. Meanwhile, in a mixing bowl, whisk together yolks with the other 35 g of sugar and the cornstarch.

5. When the milk is ready, slowly ladle about one-third of the hot milk into the egg mixture, whisking constantly.

6. Return the egg mixture back to the hot milk and bring it to a boil while whisking and cook until you see a few slow bubbles.

7. Add gelatin to the mixture once it's been pulled off the heat and pour through the sieve into a clean mixing bowl.

8. At 60°C/140°F, mix with a whisk and start adding cold butter cut into small pieces.

9. Let it cool down completely and mix delicately with whipped cream.

ASSEMBLY

1. Start by piping some crème diplomate onto a puff pastry disc.

2. Add the figs cut into quarters.

3. Add another layer of puff pastry, cream, and figs.

4. Finish with a last disc of puff pastry and some powdered sugar on top.

TARTE AU CHOCOLAT ET AU MISO-CARAMEL

Yield: 2 tarts

The traditional French chocolate tart is known for its richness and universal appeal. Alice Jaroszuk's version is decidedly smoky and adult. The miso caramel is a new spin on classic salted caramel, and the smoked ganache adds depth and complexity to the chocolate dessert's familiar flavor profile.

Smoked Ganache

500 g whipping cream

250 g dark chocolate, chopped

500 g whipping cream

30 g granulated sugar

Tart Shell

180 g unsalted butter, softened

100 g powdered sugar

1 egg

320 g all-purpose flour

Pinch salt

25 g cocoa powder

SMOKED GANACHE

1. Smoke the cream by burning some hay or small wood pieces in a pot, pouring hot cream over them, and letting them infuse for 1 hour, covered, at room temperature.

2. Afterwards, strain smoked cream and boil it.

3. Pour over chopped dark chocolate and mix well.

4. Finish by adding sugar and the rest of the cold cream.

5. Mix well and refrigerate with a cling film on top for at least 6 hours.

TART SHELL

1. Using a stand mixer fitted with the paddle attachment, combine softened butter with powdered sugar and mix on medium speed until smooth.

2. Mix in 1 egg. Stop the mixer and scrape down the sides of the bowl with a rubber spatula.

3. Add the flour, salt, and cocoa powder all at once and mix on low speed until combined. Mix only to combine; don't overwork it.

4. Wrap the dough in cling film and chill in the refrigerator for at least 1 hour.

Continued...

5. When cooled down, roll the pastry down and place it inside a 30-centimeter tart pan. Place it in the refrigerator to cool down for at least 1 hour.

6. Bake tart shells for around 15 minutes at 180°C/350°F.

CACAO FRANGIPANE

Cacao Frangipane

220 g unsalted butter, softened

200 g powdered sugar

250 g almond flour/meal

45 g cocoa powder

4 large eggs

1. In the bowl of a stand mixer fitted with paddle attachment, beat the softened butter on medium speed until creamy. Add powdered sugar, almond flour, and cocoa powder.

2. When thoroughly combined, add eggs in a slow stream. Mix until light and fluffy.

3. Transfer the cream into a pastry piping bag. Pipe the frangipane onto the baked tart shell and bake for 10 minutes more at 170°C/330°F.

MISO CARAMEL

Miso Caramel

15 g water

60 g glucose/light corn syrup

225 g granulated sugar

215 g whipping cream

135 g salted butter, cold

70 g miso

1. Put water, glucose syrup, and sugar in a pot (in that order). Start on a low heat and let it melt.

2. Once melted, turn up the heat to medium to get a nice caramel color.

3. Heat the cream and deglaze the caramel with it (off the heat). Be careful, as it might get bubbly.

4. Mix well and continue to cook it over medium heat for 5 minutes more.

5. Once cooked, transfer to a clean bowl and add cold butter to lower the temperature of the caramel.

6. When at 40°C/104°F, add miso and mix well.

7. Spread an even layer on top of the baked frangipane.

ASSEMBLY

1. Whip up the ganache in a stand mixer until soft peaks form.

2. Pipe it onto a tart shell completely cooled down.

3. Sprinkle with some Maldon salt.

CAFE BESALU

5909 24th Avenue NW
Seattle, WA 98107

This Seattle-based bakery specializes in handmade pastries and seasonal sweet and savory treats. For *The French Bakery*, they offer a savory zucchini galette as well as a sweet passion fruit tart.

TARTE AUX FRUITS DE LA PASSION

The slightly acidic nature of passion fruit is perfectly balanced with the addition of Italian meringue in this recipe. The sablé shell serves as a sturdy container while also adding density and richness.

Passion Fruit Cream

Yield: One 8-inch tart, or five 2.5-inch small tarts

380 g condensed milk

300 g water

⅛ teaspoon salt

2 egg yolks

30 g cornstarch

100 g passion fruit concentrate

PASSION FRUIT CREAM

1. In a saucepan, dissolve the condensed milk in the water; add salt.

2. Reserve about one-fourth of the cold milk mixture in a small bowl and heat the rest until steamy.

3. To the reserved milk, add egg yolks and cornstarch and whisk until no lumps of cornstarch remain.

4. Once the milk in the pot is steamy, add half to the egg yolk mixture, then put everything back in the pot.

5. Set over medium heat and whisk until it thickens.

6. Once it reaches bubble point, lower the heat and keep it there for 1 minute, constantly whisking.

7. Let cool in the pot, whisking every so often to release some of the steam.

8. Once it's only warm to the touch, whisk in the passion fruit concentrate until no lumps remain.

Pâte Sablée Shells

Yield: Two 8-inch tarts or ten 2.5-inch tarts

225 g butter, softened

135 g powdered sugar

¾ teaspoon salt

55 g eggs, beaten (about 1 large egg)

390 g pastry flour (low-gluten flour)

PÂTE SABLÉE SHELLS

1. In a stand mixer, cream butter, powdered sugar, and salt on low speed until creamy and no chunks of butter remain, about 3 minutes.

2. Slowly drizzle in beaten eggs, one bit at a time, scraping the bowl between each addition. Mix to combine until emulsified.

Italian Meringue

Yield: One 8-inch tart or 5 small tarts

120 g granulated sugar

30 g water

60 g egg whites

Pinch salt

Pinch cream of tartar (optional)

Continued...

3. Add flour in two batches, scraping the bowl well between each addition. Mix on low just until combined; do not overmix.

4. Dump dough onto an un-floured surface, divide into two portions, flatten each portion into a disc, and wrap in plastic wrap. You can freeze the dough at this point.

5. Chill at least 2 hours before rolling, using as little flour as possible. If the dough is cold enough, scraps can be rerolled right away.

6. To roll the dough: Butter an 8-inch tart pan with a removable bottom or an 8-inch tart ring. Roll out chilled dough on a floured surface to a 12-inch round, lifting and turning dough occasionally to free from the surface. If the dough is sticking, you can release it using a large offset spatula. If it sticks too much, then it's too warm; chill as needed. Turn the dough into the tart pan or tart ring, making sure to press the dough into the edges very well. Seal any cracks in the dough. Trim overhang to ½ inch. Pierce the crust all over with a fork before baking. Alternatively, if using a ring (with no bottom), you can bake on a mesh silicone mat, no piercing necessary. Chill for at least 1 hour before baking.

7. Bake in a 165°C/325°F preheated oven for 15 to 20 minutes (10 to 15 minutes for smaller tarts), or until golden brown.

ITALIAN MERINGUE

1. Whisk sugar and water in a pot and set over high heat. Once this syrup starts bubbling, do not stir or touch it, or you'll risk the syrup forming crystals.

2. In the meantime, on medium speed, whip egg whites, salt, and cream of tartar in the stand mixer using the whip attachment. You want the whites to get foamy but not whipped to any sort of peak before the syrup is ready.

3. Once the syrup reaches 115°C/240°F, immediately remove from heat and slowly drizzle onto whipping whites.

4. Increase the speed of the mixer to medium high, and whip until the meringue is glossy and beginning to ball up inside the whisk and the bowl feels body temperature, about 8 minutes. Use immediately.

ASSEMBLY

1. Spoon cream onto baked shell (or shells).

2. Smooth surface with an offset spatula.

3. Decorate with Italian meringue. Using a pastry bag and your favorite nozzle is optional.

4. Torch for a toasty finish and decorate with edible flowers if desired.

GALETTE AUX COURGES

Savory galettes are a welcome addition to any summer meal. Cafe Besalu's version includes zucchini and ricotta and is filling enough on its own but ideal with a light side salad and glass of rosé.

Puff Pastry

225 g water

25 g white vinegar

125 g pastry flour

75 g all-purpose flour

100 g einkorn flour

200 g whole wheat pastry flour

2 teaspoon salt

50 g unsalted butter, melted

400 g high-fat unsalted butter

Ricotta Tarragon Filling

500 g ricotta

1 tablespoon tarragon, finely chopped

¼ teaspoon salt

Zest of 2 lemons

PUFF PASTRY

1. Mix water and vinegar.

2. In the bowl of a stand mixer, mix dry ingredients. With a dough hook, mix the dry ingredients with half the wet mix for 30 seconds. Add butter and the rest of the water, reserving a small amount. Mix 30 seconds, scrape bottom of the bowl, then mix another 5 seconds. If it seems dry, add the rest of the water. Mix until it just comes together.

3. Turn onto work surface and knead lightly by hand until no dry flour remains, forming into a boule. Place in a greased bowl, seam side down. Slash a cross at the top of the boule with a sharp knife. Cover with plastic wrap and leave overnight in the refrigerator.

4. Make a butter block with high fat butter, 1 cm thick. Refrigerate until firm but pliable.

5. Roll dough into a circle big enough to encase the butter block. Wrap butter block with dough, folding over 4 sides, like an envelope. Push dough edges and seam shut.

6. Roll dough in one direction until it's 9 mm thick. Fold the dough into thirds like a letter. Wrap and freeze for 15 minutes or refrigerate for an hour. Roll perpendicular to the first fold until it's 9 mm thick again. Fold again like a letter. Wrap and freeze/refrigerate. Repeat 3 more times for a total of 5 folds. Refrigerate overnight.

7. Roll the dough until it's about 4 mm thick, stretching in every direction, so that it covers a 9x13 sheet pan. Relax the dough and then cut the edges using a very sharp knife, taking care not to drag the knife, to allow all the layers to puff. Slash the edges about an inch inward with a sharp knife to create the middle that will be filled. (Don't cut all the way through, though.) Pierce the middle with a fork. Chill for about 30 minutes.

8. Preheat the oven to 190°C/375°F. Parbake the puff rectangle for about 30 minutes, until it's just starting to show some color.

RICOTTA TARRAGON FILLING

1. Mix all ingredients in a bowl until thoroughly combined.

ASSEMBLY

1. Spread ricotta filling on parbaked galette.

2. Sprinkle grated Gruyère over the entire surface, including edges.

3. Arrange thinly sliced zucchini; sprinkle with salt and pepper.

4. Decorate with zucchini blossoms, if available, before baking.

BISTRO LA FLORAISON

7637 Wydown Boulevard
Clayton, MO 63105

Bistro La Floraison is a petite French bistro and wine bar based in St. Louis, Missouri. It serves modern takes on classic cuisine in a sophisticated, intimate space with a small bar and outdoor terrace. Their contributions to *The French Bakery* include a classic gougère, as well as a French onion *financier*, a savory spin on a classic small treat.

BISTRO LA FLORAISON'S GOUGÈRES WITH GRUYÈRE MOUSSE

Yield: 12 gougères (35 grams each)

"There is no better way to start an evening at Bistro La Floraison than with an order of our lighter-than-air gougères and a glass of champagne. We serve these traditional French hors d'oeuvres with a decadent Gruyère mousse for dipping, adding an additional pop of cheese with each bite. Most guests refuse to let us clear the mousse from the table until every last bite has been savored. For this recipe we suggest stuffing the gougères with the cheese mousse for easy serving at a party. However you enjoy them, they will be delicious."
—Tara Galina, co-owner of Bistro La Floraison and Take Root Hospitality

Gougères

71 g whole milk

77 g water

76 g whole unsalted butter

2 g kosher salt

99 g all-purpose flour

25 g grated Parmesan

150 g eggs

Gruyère Mousse

400 g heavy whipping cream

200 g grated Gruyère cheese

Sea salt

Sherry vinegar

GOUGÈRES

1. In a medium saucepan, bring milk, water, butter, and salt to a simmer. Whisk in flour. Once flour is homogenous, use a wooden spoon to continuously stir the mixture (known as pâte à choux dough). Cook over medium-high heat until a slight skin forms on the bottom of the pot and dough pulls away easily from the sides of the pot.

2. Move hot choux dough to a stand mixer and mix on medium high to cool down the dough slightly until it feels just above warm. Add the Parmesan then the eggs one at a time until all eggs are added and the mixture is homogeneous.

3. Line a baking sheet with parchment paper and coat with cooking spray. Preheat oven to 180°C/350°F (convection setting is preferred).

4. Place mixture in piping bags. Pipe onto trays to the size of a silver dollar, leaving an inch between each. Bake immediately or freeze at this stage and bake at a later time. Bake for 10 minutes, then rotate and bake for another 10 minutes, depending on color and doneness. Rotate and bake for another 10 minutes. You are looking for them to rise into puffs and be golden brown.

5. Consume right away or hold them at room temperature and flash in a 180°C/350°F oven for 2 minutes to reheat and crisp up.

GRUYÈRE MOUSSE

1. Bring heavy whipping cream to a simmer in a pot.

2. Pour hot cream into a blender; blend on high while adding cheese until homogenous. Season to taste with salt and sherry vinegar.

3. Place cheese fondue into an iSi canister, charge with one cream charge, and shake vigorously.

ASSEMBLY

1. Once gougères are baked, flip them upside down, make a small hole in the bottom, and fill them with the mousse.

KRISTIN BRANGWYNNE

The Conrad Nashville
1620 West End Avenue
Nashville, TN 37203

Chef Kristin Brangwynne grew up in a small town in Massachusetts. From a young age she was fascinated with all things beautiful, wanting to pursue a career in art. With more and more exposure in the kitchen, helping with desserts for family events and birthdays, she saw how much happiness and satisfaction people received from tasting these dishes. She decided that this was the direction she wanted: a career in creating beautiful desserts while bringing more happiness into the world.

Chef Kristin attended the Culinary Institute of America in Hyde Park, New York, where she graduated with an associate's degree in baking and pastry, as well as a bachelor's degree in food business management with a concentration in advanced pastry. She then started working as a pastry manager in training at Gaylord Opryland Resort in Nashville, Tennessee. Starting at such a large property helped her develop the skills needed to create beautiful dishes on a high-volume scale. From there, Chef Kristin participated in her first hotel opening, Grand Hyatt Nashville, in 2020, giving her menu development and hotel start-up exposure and introducing a knack for recipe writing and menu design.

The skills she acquired from her schooling and previous experience helped make multiple career dreams possible, from publishing her first pastry book, *Equinox*, in January of 2022 to being the pastry chef to open the Conrad Nashville just a few months later. She creates her own recipes, and she and her team supply all the desserts found on the property, from the two restaurant outlets to catering functions and amenities. Chef Kristin is on track to learn and grow as much as she can in this industry. Every experience is an opportunity for her to spread a little more sweetness into the world.

PETITS CHOUX À LA MANGUE

*A denser and more indulgent version of the light and airy chou-
quettes, these mango-and-basil-cream-filled choux pastries are
an exotic take on a profiterole. The addition of brown sugar craquelin adds both style and substance to these two-bite desserts.*

Pâte à Choux

240 g water

92 g butter

4 g salt

170 g all-purpose flour

170 g eggs

Brown Sugar Craquelin

50 g unsalted butter

55 g brown sugar

1 g salt

65 g bread flour

PÂTE À CHOUX

1. Heat water, butter, and salt in a saucepan; bring to a boil.

2. Add flour; cook until a film forms on the bottom of the pan.

3. Transfer into a mixing bowl with a paddle attachment. Paddle to cool down.

4. Add in eggs until desired consistency is achieved.

5. Pipe on Silpat-lined trays, place on craquelin, and bake at 190°C/375°F.

BROWN SUGAR CRAQUELIN

1. Combine all ingredients in a mixing bowl with a paddle attachment. Paddle until smooth and combined.

2. Spread between 2 Silpats until thin and even. Freeze until solid.

3. Peel off top Silpat and punch out circles slightly larger than the piped choux. Place craquelin discs on top of choux.

4. Bake at 190°C/375°F for 15 to 20 minutes, until puffs are golden.

Continued...

Mango Compote

285 g mango, peeled
and small diced

90 g water

75 g granulated sugar

½ teaspoon lemon juice

11 g cornstarch

Basil Crémeux

500 g heavy cream

15 basil leaves

1 sheet gelatin

200 g white chocolate

MANGO COMPOTE

1. Combine mango, 45 g of water, sugar, and lemon juice in a pot.

2. Cook until the mango has softened.

3. Combine the remaining water and cornstarch in a separate bowl to create a slurry.

4. Add the slurry to the mango mixture.

5. Cook until the mixture has thickened. Remove from heat and let cool down completely before use.

BASIL CRÉMEUX

1. Combine heavy cream and basil leaves in a pot. Bring to a simmer. Let steep for 15 to 20 minutes.

2. Bloom gelatin in ice water; set aside.

3. Immersion blend basil leaves into cream. Strain out solids and return to the heat.

4. Bring basil cream to a boil. Remove from heat and stir in bloomed gelatin.

5. Pour mixture over white chocolate. Emulsify until smooth.

6. Let mixture chill for 4 to 6 hours before whipping to stiff peaks.

ASSEMBLY

1. Slice the tops off the baked pâte à choux.

2. Fill the bottom of the cream puff with the cooled mango compote.

3. Whip basil cream to stiff peaks.

4. In a pastry bag fitted with a large star tip, pipe a rosette of basil cream on top of the mango compote.

5. Place the cap back on the cream puff.

6. Dust with powdered sugar before serving.

ALLIANCE BAKERY

1736 W Division Street
Chicago, IL 60622

Alliance Bakery is a renowned Chicago-based pastry and dessert shop situated in Wicker Park. The recipes they share with *The French Bakery*—a walnut sablé–based Sophia and a raspberry-rosé dome—are examples of the shop's elegance and finesse.

SOPHIA

The density and crunch of dried fruits and walnut sablé are matched with smooth and velvety mascarpone mousse in a dessert that balances slightly sour and sweet thanks to the balsamic vinegar reduction. Although perfect for any season, the fruits and nuts would be a perfect end to an autumn meal.

Walnut Sablé

225 g butter, softened

100 g granulated sugar

70 g brown sugar

4 g salt

100 g egg yolks

250 g all-purpose flour

10 g baking powder

80 g finely chopped walnuts

Caramelized Dried Fruits

100 g balsamic vinegar

170 g dried apricots

70 g dried black mission figs

58 g dried cherries

42 g chopped pistachios

42 g chopped walnuts

130 g granulated sugar

40 g water

½ piece vanilla bean

1 g salt

50 g unsalted butter

WALNUT SABLÉ

1. Cream butter, sugars, and salt.

2. Add egg yolks to combine.

3. Combine all remaining dry ingredients and then slowly add to the butter and egg mix.

4. Cool for 24 hours.

5. Roll out until 5 mm thick.

6. Cut out 8 cm circles.

CARAMELIZED DRIED FRUITS

1. Measure out 100 g of balsamic vinegar into a saucepan and reduce by half over medium-high heat.

2. Dice all fruits into ⅛-inch cubes.

3. Add fruits to a saucepan filled with water over high heat and blanch for 2 minutes.

4. Drain and rinse under cold water for 2 to 3 minutes in a colander.

5. In a separate saucepan, cook sugar, water, and vanilla bean over medium-high heat until caramelization occurs.

6. Add salt and butter.

7. Quickly add the blanched fruits and stir in balsamic reduction.

Continued...

Mascarpone Mousse

85 g water

40 g milk powder

150 g granulated sugar

45 g egg yolk (2 to 3 eggs)

6 g gelatin leaves

320 g mascarpone cheese

400 g heavy cream

White Chocolate Glaze

250 g milk

80 g corn syrup

8 g gelatin sheets

600 g Valrhona Ivoire white chocolate

MASCARPONE MOUSSE

1. Mix water, milk powder, sugar, and yolks together in a mixing bowl.

2. Place over a water bath and whisk until thick, 5 to 6 minutes.

3. Add hydrated gelatin leaves.

4. Fold in mascarpone cheese.

5. Whip heavy cream to soft peaks and fold into the mascarpone mixture.

6. Pour into 8 cm flan rings.

7. Top with caramelized dried fruits and freeze.

WHITE CHOCOLATE GLAZE

1. Bring milk and corn syrup to a boil.

2. Add hydrated gelatin and white chocolate.

3. Use an immersion blender to emulsify.

4. Cool for at least 24 hours.

ASSEMBLY

1. Unmold mousse from rings.

2. Glaze with white chocolate glaze.

3. Transfer onto a baked walnut sablé and garnish with caramelized dried fruits.

ALEXANDRA PUGLISI

Le Coucou
138 Lafayette Street
New York, NY 10013

Alexandra Puglisi grew up in Upstate New York, baking with her great-grandmother for the local newspaper. Helping her develop recipes eventually led Alex down the culinary track. She is now a professional pastry chef and avid home baker with experience from top New York restaurants. She spent the bulk of her career as a pastry sous chef at L'Atelier de Joël Robuchon in New York City. During the pandemic, Alex launched a dessert pop-up called 32nd & Tart. She also worked as a pastry sous chef at the acclaimed Gabriel Kreuther Restaurant and is now Executive Pastry Chef of Le Coucou in Lower Manhattan.

TARTE AU CITRON

A classic French dessert for citrus lovers the world over. This recipe is about balancing out the tart lemon curd by combining it with a rich sablé crust, sweet biscuit chiffon, and creamy vanilla Chantilly. Combined in one bite, you have the perfect finish to a meal that pleases every taste bud.

Lemon Curd

Yield: 1 tart

112 g lemon juice

112 g granulated sugar

6 eggs

225 g butter

LEMON CURD

1. On a bain-marie, heat lemon juice, sugar, and eggs until thickened, stirring with a whisk the entire time.

2. Remove from heat and add in the butter a little at a time while whisking.

3. Once all the butter is incorporated, cover the surface with plastic wrap and allow to cool completely in the refrigerator.

Biscuit Chiffon

Yield: 7 pieces, 1 per tart

105 g egg yolk

105 g oil

110 g water

6 g vanilla extract

112 g granulated sugar

232 g all-purpose flour

9 g baking powder

112 g sugar

255 g egg whites

BISCUIT CHIFFON

1. Combine egg yolk, oil, water, and vanilla extract.

2. Combine all the dry ingredients and the first amount of sugar. Add to the wet ingredients and whisk until smooth.

3. Whip the egg whites and second amount of sugar slowly until firm (about 12 minutes on a standing mixer).

4. Fold the whites into the batter in thirds until incorporated.

5. Divide into 1,000 g and spread onto full sheet trays lined with parchment paper.

6. Bake at 190°C/375°F for 4 minutes and then rotate for another 4 minutes.

7. Allow the cake to cool and then cut with a rectangle tart cutter.

8. Reserve these rectangles until ready to assemble the tart.

Continued...

Sablé Breton

Yield: 10 pieces

550 g unsalted
butter, softened

180 g powdered sugar

20 g egg yolk

3 g fleur de sel

500 g flour

100 g cornstarch

Vanilla Chantilly

2000 g heavy cream

200 g granulated sugar

2 vanilla beans, split

20 g gelatin

SABLÉ BRETON

1. In a stand mixer, paddle butter and powdered sugar until well combined.

2. Add the egg yolk in 3 additions, scraping after each addition.

3. Add the dry ingredients all at once and pulse just until combined.

4. Portion the sablé out into 350 g balls and roll between two sheets of parchment paper until ½-inch thick. Refrigerate these sheets of dough until cool.

5. Peel away the parchments and cut the sablé with a rectangle tart cutter.

6. Place one of these sablés on a sheet tray lined with parchment paper and place a rectangle tart mold around the outside.

7. Bake at 165°C/325°F for 10 to 12 minutes or until a deep golden brown. Reserve until ready to assemble the tart.

VANILLA CHANTILLY

1. Heat half the cream with the sugar and the vanilla beans.

2. Once boiling, add the bloomed gelatin and pour over the other half of the cream.

3. Immersion blend and then portion into quart containers. Allow to cool overnight.

ASSEMBLY

1. Grab the sablé Breton with the rectangular tart mold around it. Spread a little bit of lemon curd on the bottom, just enough to allow the biscuit chiffon to stick to the cookie.

2. Place a biscuit chiffon over the sablé Breton. Top with the lemon curd and, using a small offset, smooth out the top. Allow this tart to sit in the refrigerator for 2 to 3 hours before unmolding.

3. To unmold, grab a small offset spatula and dip it in warm water, run the offset along the edges of the tart to release it from the mold, and then slowly lift up.

4. Whip a quart of the vanilla Chantilly until stiff peaks form and place into a pastry bag fitted with a large rose tip.

5. Pipe lines diagonally along the entire surface of the tart. It's okay if the Chantilly goes over the edges of the tart; you can trim this off later.

6. Reserve the tart in the refrigerator.

7. Get a pot of boiling water, a cutting board, and a knife ready. Using the hot knife, trim off all the excess cream until you have nice sharp corners and edges on your tart. Now cut 1.5-inch pieces, the tart should yield 7 portions.

8. Finish with a little fresh citrus zest and enjoy!

CHEZ NOIR

5th Avenue between Dolores
and San Carlos Streets
Carmel-by-the-Sea, CA 93921

Chez Noir is a European-inspired bistro in Carmel-by-the-Sea, California. The name pays subtle and sophisticated homage to the family who owns and runs it. Chef Jonny Black and co-owner Monique Black's Chez Noir means "the Blacks' home" or "at the Blacks'" in French.

The restaurant is both elevated and community-driven, featuring French- and Spanish-inspired cuisine that is rooted in coastal California tradition. The husband-and-wife team consider it their passion project after years of combined experience in the hospitality industry.

Jonny Black was born in the Bay Area and raised in Virginia, leading him to be exposed to regional and coastal cuisine at a very young age. He received a full scholarship to The Culinary Institute of America in Hyde Park, graduating with honors in 2007 before moving to New York City to become an opening member of the team at Allen & Delancey and Corton, and then chef de partie at Per Se.

He has spent time staging at Noma, Relae, In de Wulf, and The Clove Club in Europe, and worked as chef de cuisine at Governor in Brooklyn and Quince in San Francisco. He became executive sous chef at Pineapple & Pearls in Washington, DC, and then executive chef for the Crenn Dining Group in San Francisco. In this role, alongside Chef Dominique Crenn, he saw Atelier Crenn earn its third Michelin star and Bar Crenn earn its first.

In 2019 Chef Black relocated from San Francisco to Monterey Bay, assuming the role of executive chef at Post Ranch Inn in Big Sur, California. With a vision for opening his own family-run restaurant in the tight-knit community, he spent nearly two years observing the inner workings of the region's dining culture and gaining an appreciation for the hyper-regional seafood and produce available throughout the Monterey Peninsula.

Co-owner Monique is originally from Washington, DC, but began her career as a line cook in New York City. It was at restaurants Colonie and Governor that she discovered the magic of an open-kitchen format and enjoyed the interaction she had with guests. When Governor closed due to Hurricane Sandy, Black began contemplating a shift to front-of-house, ultimately relocating to San Francisco to work at Quince. She remained at the restaurant for three and a half years before relocating to Washington, DC, where she joined the front-of-house team at two-Michelin-starred Pineapple & Pearls in Capitol Hill. Eventually, Black returned with her growing family to the Bay Area and joined the small front-of-house team at Coi, which had just earned its third Michelin star.

Taking a brief sabbatical from hospitality to support her family, she and her husband relocated to Carmel-by-the-Sea with the vision of developing their own family-run restaurant.

Chez Noir offers its guests the everyday luxury of thoughtfully prepared, seasonal fare and the warm hospitality of a family-run restaurant.

The menu includes baked goods, charcuterie, preserved produce, dry-aged fish, and fresh pastas. For *The French Bakery*, they are proud to share sweet treats such as their chocolate tart and canelé, as well as a savory pâté en croûte.

CHOCOLATE SABAYON TART "L'AMBROISE"

Calling all chocolate lovers! This tart, which highlights a dark chocolate sabayon base, is the ultimate in chocolate desserts. Vanilla-bourbon ice cream adds a creamy and light contrast to the rich filling.

Sweet Tart Dough

Yield: One 8-inch tart

150 g granulated sugar

240 g butter

100 g eggs

420 g cake flour

Pinch kosher salt

Dark Chocolate Sabayon Base

Yield: 4 tarts

210 g heavy cream

195 g 70% Valrhona chocolate

3 eggs

9 egg yolks

75 g granulated sugar

23 g cake flour

Vanilla Bean and Bourbon Ice Cream

200 g granulated sugar

200 g egg yolks

660 g whole milk

180 g heavy cream

4 vanilla beans, scraped

SWEET TART DOUGH

1. Combine the sugar and butter until the mixture has a pomade texture.

2. Add the eggs one by one until well blended.

3. Finally add the flour and salt. Mix it into smooth dough.

4. Once done, wrap it in a plastic film and allow it to rest in the refrigerator for about 3 hours before using.

5. When chilled, roll the dough to 2 mm thickness and make the tart.

6. Punch a few holes in it and blind bake it at 200°C/400°F for 12 minutes.

DARK CHOCOLATE SABAYON BASE

1. Bring the cream to just below a simmer, then remove from heat.

2. Add chocolate and allow to melt; mix until smooth and set aside.

3. Whip eggs and yolks with the sugar into a foam over a double boiler until you obtain a ribbon texture. Sift flour into the eggs and, finally, fold in the chocolate mixture.

4. Pour the sabayon into the tart and bake for 3 minutes at 190°C/375°F. The point of the tart is to actually under-bake it so the center stays soft and runny.

VANILLA BEAN AND BOURBON ICE CREAM

1. Whip sugar and egg yolks together.

2. Whisk in whole milk and heavy cream.

3. Add to a sous vide bag along with the scraped vanilla and empty pods, then vacuum seal. Bag with vanilla bean.

4. Steam at 85°C/185°F for 1 hour.

5. Strain through a chinois.

6. Set into Pacojet containers and freeze fully overnight.

NOTE: Chez Noir creates their ice cream using the sous-vide method. This could also be prepared using the traditional crème anglaise, or custard-making, method.

CHEZ NOIR'S GUINEA HEN AND PORK PÂTÉ EN CROÛTE

As a starter or main course, this pâté en croûte is the perfect addition to any meal. Containing pork, shallots, and garlic, the farce is sure to please even those who have never tried pâté before. The choux pastry dough is added as a binding agent inside the farce, while the shortcrust dough bakes to a golden brown on the outside.

1500 g guinea hen meat

300 g guinea hen livers

500 g pork butt

1000 g pork fatback

200 g shallots, sliced thin

150 g garlic clove

9 g pink salt

36 g kosher salt

4 g four spice

125 g Xerez vinegar (split with half honey vinegar)

125 g cognac

200 g Pâte à Choux

Pâte à Choux

500 g water

250 g butter

275 g all-purpose flour

500 g whole eggs

1. Marinate all ingredients except Pâte à Choux for 6 to 8 hours.

2. Separate pork fat and grind through medium dice twice.

3. Grind pork through a small dice twice with guinea hen liver and guinea hen meat. Chill everything.

4. Beat with a mixer paddle until well incorporated. Add fat and paté a choux and beat until homogenous. Chill.

PÂTE À CHOUX

1. Heat water and butter to a light simmer.

2. Add flour and cook until most of the moisture has evaporated.

3. Add to the stand mixer and paddle until the bowl feels just warm.

4. Add in eggs one at a time until fully combined. Set aside.

Continued...

Shortcrust Pastry Dough

1000 g all-purpose flour

25 g salt

250 g diced butter, chilled

160 g water, chilled

4 eggs, chilled

250 g shredded butter, chilled

SHORTCRUST PASTRY DOUGH

1. Add flour, salt, and diced butter to a stand mixer with the paddle attachment. Paddle slowly until it reaches the texture of almond flour.

2. Add chilled water and eggs into the dough and loosely combine.

3. Quickly add in the shredded butter and lightly mix until the dough fully forms.

4. Chill dough and roll out evenly until 2 to 3 mm thick.

ASSEMBLY

1. Once the dough is rolled out and your pâte farce is chilled, cut a rectangle of dough that will fit your pâte mold, around 13x15 inches.

2. Lay into the mold and place 2 squares' worth of dough that can cover the ends. Slightly chill.

3. Press 2000 g of finished pâte farce evenly through the pâte mold lined with the dough. All components should be chilled during assembly.

4. Egg wash lightly, seal the top onto the dough, and crimp all of the edges, making sure it is sealed tightly. Chill and clean up the edges with a paring knife.

5. Make 3 holes in the top of the en croute to help with airflow during baking.

6. Egg wash 3 times every 20 minutes to allow for the wash to directly soak into the dough.

7. Let rest for 1 hour.

8. Bake at 215°C/420°F for 10 minutes.

9. Turn the oven down to 180°C/350°F and bake for another 40 minutes.

10. Chill overnight.

11. Set with your preferred gelee the following day.

SAMANTHA BAUM

Samantha Baum is a pastry chef and food writer based in the Bay Area. After having worked as chef de partie for Ad Hoc in Yountville, California, and Ai Fiori in New York, she became pastry sous chef at Monsieur Benjamin in San Francisco and then Tartine. For the past five years, she has been pastry sous chef for Salesforce in downtown San Francisco.

GALETTE AUX CERISES ET RHUBARBE

This is Baum's cherry mulberry galette with rhubarb and sesame rye crust. This recipe is best when using in-season cherries. In Baum's words: "If you're not making galettes in the summer, you're doing it all wrong! Cherry season is short and sweet, so be sure to grab some fresh cherries at your local farmer's market, along with other spring delights."

Cream Cheese Pie Dough

115 g cold unsalted butter, cubed and frozen for at least 30 minutes

130 g all-purpose flour, plus more as needed

50 g rye flour

3 g salt

5 g brown sugar

1 g baking powder

90 g cream cheese

22 g ice water

7 g apple cider vinegar

15 g sesame seeds

CREAM CHEESE PIE DOUGH

1. Place the flours, salt, sugar, and baking powder in the food processor with the metal blade and then add the frozen butter cubes, pulsing until none of the butter pieces are larger than the size of a pea.

2. Cut the cream cheese into 3 or 4 pieces and add it to the flour. Process for about 20 seconds or until the mixture resembles a coarse meal.

3. Remove the cover and add the water and vinegar. Pulse a few times until just incorporated. Add the sesame seeds and pulse to incorporate. The mixture will look crumbly, but when pressed together in your hand it should hold its shape.

4. Dump the mixture out onto a lightly floured surface and knead the dough into a flattened disc. If you need to add a touch more water while kneading, do so, but use caution as you do not want the dough to become wet.

5. Wrap the dough in plastic wrap and place in the refrigerator for at least an hour but ideally overnight.

6. The next day, roll out the dough to about an 11-inch/28-cm circle. Cut the dough into a perfect circle using either a tart ring mold or a bowl and knife.

7. Place the dough circle onto a parchment- or Silpat-lined baking sheet and place it in the freezer while prepping the fruit.

Continued...

Cherry Galette Filling

430 g cherries, pitted and sliced in half

115 g mulberries

225 g rhubarb, chopped

75 g brown sugar

20 g flour

Juice and zest of 1 lemon

5 g sea salt

Assembly

20 g almond flour

13 g granulated sugar, plus more for topping as needed

Egg or heavy cream

CHERRY GALETTE FILLING

1. Heat oven to 190°C/375°F.

2. In a medium-size bowl, combine the prepped cherries, mulberries, rhubarb, brown sugar, flour, lemon juice, lemon zest, and salt.

3. Mix the fruit to coat evenly with the sugar mixture. Be careful not to smash the fruits too much.

ASSEMBLY

1. Pull the chilled dough round out of the freezer.

2. Mix the almond flour and granulated sugar together. Sprinkle the mixture over the chilled dough round, leaving a 1.5-inch/4 cm rim around the edge of the dough.

3. Place cherry filling onto the center of dough over the almond-sugar mixture, leaving the 1.5-inch/4 cm border around the edge.

4. Make sure the dough has thawed slightly and won't crack when folded. Fold the edge up and over the filling, overlapping and creating pleats all the way around.

5. Whisk an egg, if using. Brush the surface of the dough with heavy cream or egg wash.

6. Sprinkle the top of the galette (especially the crust) with some granulated sugar.

7. Bake for about 40 to 50 minutes until the crust is golden brown and done on the bottom. Transfer to a wire rack and cool slightly before slicing.

SERVING SUGGESTION: serve with your favorite ice cream, whipped cream, or a dollop of crème fraîche.

NOTES:

- This galette recipe will work with all cherries or other stone fruits and a mixture of berries.

- The almond flour/sugar mix on the bottom of the galette is key to a crispy bottom—do not leave it out!

- Baking the sheet tray on top of a preheated pizza stone in the oven can also help achieve a crispy bottom.

CHAPTER 4

LES GÂTEAUX

Although it's popular vernacular and enough to roil the strict *Académie Française*, the word *gâteau* is used as an umbrella term for quite a few sweet things in France. There are sponge cakes called *quatre-quarts*, delicate dacquoises, charlottes, and more that fall under the "cake" category. But the term is often applied to cookies (even though many originate from shortcrust or sweet dough recipes). And for those being truly generic, the word can be used for almost anything that counts as dessert (although it should be noted that not all gâteaux or cakes are sweet). Here, we consider anything that passes as a cake, cookie, or other dessert as appropriate, although overlap with patisserie is bound to happen. Instead of fighting over semantics, we suggest taste-testing these recipes as a better use of your time!

COOKIES AU LEVAIN

Yield: 25 cookies

True to Shinya's style, these leaven cookies are rustic and more of a celebration of the whole wheat and buckwheat flour than they are of sugar and butter. Perfect to accompany a cup of tea, these leaven cookies are only slightly sweet yet rich and filling.

240 g unsalted butter, softened

260 g granulated sugar, plus more as needed

7 g fine salt

250 g leaven

250 g whole wheat flour (T80)

270 g buckwheat flour (T130)

80 g linseed

1. Add softened butter to a mixing bowl. Add the sugar and salt.

2. Add leaven, then add both flours that have been pre-mixed with the linseed.

3. Mix the dough by hand, then separate into two separate rolls.

4. Wrap the rolls in plastic wrap and refrigerate for 18 hours.

5. When ready to bake, sprinkle a baking sheet with sugar.

6. Unwrap the rolls and roll each one in sugar.

7. Cut 8 mm cookies from each roll (about 12 to 13 cookies per roll).

8. Heat oven to 170°C/340°F.

9. Bake the cookies for 25 to 30 minutes.

LAURIE ELLEN PELLICANO

Laurie Ellen Pellicano is a Jersey-born, Brooklyn-based baker, food stylist, consultant, and writer who first discovered her love for baking with an Easy-Bake. She graduated from baking by light bulb to professional baking in the Bay Area, where she attended undergrad.

Following graduation, Laurie Ellen spent her formative years working at San Francisco's Tartine Bakery. During her tenure there, she spearheaded the pastry R & D, all while leading a team of talented bakers in one of America's most respected bakeries. She was awarded a Zagat 30 under 30 award and helped to garner a James Beard Nomination for *Tartine Book No. 3*.

In addition to her consulting work, she runs a short-run cookie company that is devoted to developing cookies and snacks with seasonal ingredients of paramount quality. She is also a contributor to NYT Cooking, *Taste*, Epicurious, and Food52. When she's not traveling or behind the scenes in kitchens around the world, Laurie Ellen is in Brooklyn fostering meaningful relationships between people and food, whether it be through hosting gatherings at her home or through volunteer work in the food justice space.

Her cookies and other sweet and savory snacks can be purchased at laurieellen.com.

SABLÉS AU SAFFRON

Yield: 2 dozen 3-inch cookies

"Kashmiri saffron is the star in these luxurious golden cookies. The saffron will perfume the air with an intoxicating aroma as you mix the dough. Honey enhances the saffron's natural sweetness, lingering on the tongue with a light floral and slightly funky element. Drawing inspiration from a storied history of Indian cookies and biscuits, this recipe was a collaborative effort with the Diaspora Co. spice company, which sources South Asia's freshest heirloom and single-origin spices directly from farm partners for use in their holiday cookie tin. These make a lovely accompaniment to a warm beverage and welcome addition to any cookie tin. Granulated honey is honey that takes a solid shape and dissolves more easily, like sugar, for addition into recipes and can be found online, in health or natural food stores, and specialty markets."
—Laurie Ellen Pellicano

2 tablespoons whole milk

1 big pinch Kashmiri saffron, crushed or very finely chopped

210 g cups unbleached all-purpose flour

90 g cornstarch

½ teaspoon kosher salt

228 g unsalted butter, softened

100 g packed light brown sugar

1 tablespoon honey, preferably light and floral (such as wildflower, orange blossom, or clover)

Granulated honey, to coat

1. Heat the milk in a small pot over medium heat until just under a boil.

2. Remove from the heat, add the crushed saffron, stir, and allow to bloom and cool while you prepare the remaining ingredients.

3. In a medium bowl whisk together the flour, cornstarch, and salt. Set aside.

4. In the bowl of a stand mixer or in a large bowl with an electric hand mixer, beat the butter and sugar until just light in color and a little fluffy, about 2 to 3 minutes (add an extra 1 to 2 minutes if using a hand mixer). Add the honey, beat again to combine, then add the cooled, bloomed saffron milk, a little at a time, beating as you go until fully combined.

5. Add the flour mixture and beat on low speed until no dry streaks remain. Stop the mixer and, using a rubber spatula, fold over a few times by hand to ensure the batter is even and no pockets of flour or unmixed butter remain. The overall hue should be an even, sunny yellow; if it looks streaky, give it a few more folds. The dough should be one smooth, creamy mass and should not stick much to your hands when patted.

6. Gather the dough, wrap it in plastic, and pat it out to ½-inch thickness. Chill for at least 15 minutes.

7. Remove the dough from the refrigerator and turn it out onto a lightly floured sheet of parchment paper. Dust with a little more flour and top with another sheet of parchment. Roll the dough out until it's ¼ inch thick. Transfer your rolled dough to a sheet pan and chill until firm, about another 15 to 30 minutes.

8. While the dough is chilling, preheat the oven to 165°C/325°F and center the racks. Fill a wide, shallow bowl with granulated honey.

9. Remove the dough from the refrigerator and peel back the top layer of parchment. Cover back up with the layer of parchment, flip the dough sheet, and peel back the second layer of parchment. (This helps release the dough to make it easy to transfer to the baking sheets.) Now, with flour-dusted

cutters, cut out rounds of dough (a 2.5-inch fluted cutter works nicely here) and transfer them to the bowl with granulated honey, coat both sides gently, and transfer to parchment-lined baking sheets, spacing them 1 inch apart (cookies don't spread much).

10. Gather scraps, re-roll, and chill as before, cutting additional rounds from the scrap, or save dough for a later use. If the dough warms up and gets sticky while you are working with it, transfer it to the refrigerator or freezer to chill briefly before proceeding.

11. Bake the cookies, rotating after 8 minutes, until the edges just start to turn golden, about 11 to 13 minutes total.

12. Remove from the oven and let cool on trays.

13. Store in an airtight container for up to 1 month. (Dough can also be frozen in blocks to be rolled out and baked at a future date.)

BOUCHONS AUX CANNEBERGES

Yield: 5 dozen
1-inch cookies

"Shortbread is the cornerstone of my cookie world and is a fantastic playground for flavor. Shortbread also ages gracefully, getting better as it sits and flavors have a chance to meld together. These are a one-to-two-bite affair, exploding in your mouth with a trio of sour ingredients: cranberry, hibiscus, and sumac. Cranberry is the star, lending a brilliant color, slightly bitter tang, and distinctly American flare to these buttery cookies. I like to grind my own freeze-dried powders, but you can also find pre-ground—just be sure to use the best quality cured sumac you can find."

—Laurie Ellen Pellicano

232 g unbleached
all-purpose flour

98 g cornstarch

15 g freeze-dried
cranberry powder, sifted

6 g hibiscus powder,
sifted

6 g sumac

½ teaspoon kosher salt

228 g unsalted
butter, softened

60 g powdered sugar

Coating

100 g granulated sugar

10 g freeze-dried
cranberry powder

4 g hibiscus powder

4 g sumac

1. In a medium bowl, whisk together the flour, cornstarch, cranberry, hibiscus, sumac, and salt. Set aside.

2. In the bowl of a stand mixer, beat the butter and powdered sugar until creamy and a little fluffy, about 2 to 3 minutes (add an extra 1 to 2 minutes if using a hand mixer).

3. Stop and scrape the bowl to ensure everything is creamy, then add the flour mixture all at once and beat on low speed until no dry streaks remain.

4. Stop your mixer and use a rubber spatula to fold over a few times by hand to ensure the batter is even and no pockets of flour or unmixed butter remain. If you find any, give them a good paddle by hand or return to the mixer for 5 to 10 seconds. The dough should look homogenous, evenly pink, and should not stick much to your hands when patted.

5. Mix the coating: fill a small, wide, shallow bowl with the sugar, cranberry, hibiscus, and sumac; keep near.

6. Scoop rounded teaspoons of dough, roll into balls, and transfer them to the bowl with the coating sugar. Coat completely and transfer to parchment-lined baking sheets, spacing them 1 inch apart; cookies will not spread much. If the dough warms up and gets sticky while you are working with it, transfer it to the refrigerator or freezer

to chill briefly before proceeding. Likewise, if it is dry, cover it with a piece of plastic to keep it from drying out further. You may also want to have a small bowl of water to moisten your hands to assist in rolling the dough.

7. When sheet pans are full, transfer them to the refrigerator and chill until firm, about 15 to 30 minutes. This will keep the cookies from spreading too much while they bake, as the dough has likely warmed up a bit in your hands.

8. While the dough is chilling, preheat the oven to 165°C/325°F and center the racks.

9. Bake the cookies for a total of 15 to 18 minutes until the bottoms and edges are just starting to turn brown, rotating after 10 minutes. It's important to toggle your oven temperature if your cookies begin to color too quickly, as you want them to remain as vibrantly pink as possible. Drop the temp to 140°C/300°F if necessary.

10. Remove from the oven and let cool on trays. Store in an airtight container for up to 1 month. (Dough can also be frozen in a block to be rolled out and baked at a future date.)

NICOLETTE LOUNIBOS

Valley Bar and Bottle
487 1st Street West
Sonoma, CA 95476

Nicolette Lounibos is a chef hailing from the Bay Area. After years of honing her skills and favorite flavors, which primarily highlight fresh California produce, her fare can now be enjoyed at Valley Bar and Bottle in Sonoma, where she has developed the entire pastry program. Here, she offers a recipe for her specialty tisane-flavored cookies, perfect as an afternoon or after-dinner treat.

TISANE COOKIE

Although known for their cafés, the French are actually avid tea drinkers as well. A tisane, or herbal tea, in the evening is considered a healthy way to end the day or a particularly heavy meal. Nicolette Lounibos's tisane cookie incorporates that light and herbal flavor with a delicious and buttery cookie for perfectly balanced treat.

227 g (2 sticks) unsalted butter, softened

22.5 g 1 any ratio of the following dry herbs, ground: mint, lemon verbena, shiso, anise hyssop, makrut leaf, lemongrass

50 g powdered sugar

250 g all-purpose flour

65 g toasted Italian pistachios or hazelnuts, chopped

1 egg, beaten with 2 tablespoons water, for the wash

Turbinado sugar, for coating

1. Preheat the oven to 180°C/350°F and line a sheet tray with parchment paper.

2. In the bowl of a stand mixer fitted with the paddle attachment, combine the butter and ground tisane blend. Alternatively, if you don't have a stand mixer, you may combine ingredients in the drum of the food processor with a blade attachment.

3. Beat with paddle until light and fluffy and the color of the compound butter is vibrant and green. If using a food processor, pulse until ingredients are just combined, about 5 to 7 pulses.

4. Sift powdered sugar into butter mixture and beat until well incorporated. For the food processor, pulse an additional 3 to 4 times.

5. Add flour, nuts, and salt into the butter-and-sugar mixture. Using the same paddle attachment on low speed, fold until well incorporated, scraping down the sides of the bowl with a rubber spatula if necessary. For the food processor, begin by adding the flour and salt, pulsing 5 to 7 times or until incorporated. Fold in nuts at the final step and pulse 3 to 4 times.

6. Prepare a sheet of plastic wrap and place dough in the center.

7. Using the plastic wrap and your hands, form a 2.5-inch log, twisting the ends of plastic wrap so the dough packet resembles a Tootsie Roll.

8. Using the twisted ends, roll the log away from your body to smooth the sides.

9. Refrigerate for a minimum of 2 hours before baking.

10. When you are ready to bake, with pastry brush, brush all sides of the log with egg wash and roll in turbinado sugar.

11. Cut off the ends and cut into ½-inch rounds and place them on a sheet pan lined with parchment.

12. Bake at 180°C/350°F for 4 minutes, rotate the pan, and bake another 4 minutes or until the edges are well browned but the center is green.

PITCHOUN!

545 S Olive Street
Los Angeles, CA 90013

8500 Beverly Boulevard #103
Los Angeles, CA 90048

Pitchoun! is a French bakery, pastry shop, and café originally located in downtown Los Angeles. In 2018 they opened their second location in the West Side, and they expect to open a third LA location in 2023.

Their specialties include bread, pastries, sandwiches, and salads, as well as an array of savory and sweet treats.

Pitchoun! is based on family. The owners, French couple Fabienne and Frédéric Souliès, are both bread and pastry lovers. Frédéric comes from a long line of French family bakers and farmers and inherited a love of organic, home-grown food and homemade bakes like those they offer in-store. After having completed university-level studies, Frédéric's passion for cooking brought him to the National School of Baking in Paris. Fabienne, on her side, inherited the knowledge of Mediterranean cuisine with an Italian twist from her parents. Frédéric oversees the production and management while Fabienne takes care of marketing and sales.

The word *pitchoun* originates from Provençal, a language still spoken by some in the Provence region of France. It means "kiddo" or "you little thing," and is often used affectionately toward children. Frédéric was called pitchoun by his grandparents and great-grandparents growing up. His great-grandparents themselves were bakery owners in Agen, and playing in their bakery as a child was what led him to choosing this sentimental name for the couple's business.

All of Pitchoun's items are created in-house, handmade every day from scratch, even jams and chocolates, and in small batches. Pitchoun! prides themselves in delivering an authentic French Mediterranean cuisine; most dishes are made from Souliès' family recipes. Pitchoun! has received several awards for its hand-crafted baked items, including being a nominee at the Best Croissant in Los Angeles 2016 Competition; Best Dessert award 2017; Best Baguette of LA nominee 2016 Competition; and Best Baguette of LA 2019 Competition Grand winner, winning all three bread awards, including Best Baguette, Best Specialty bread, and Best Bread.

BISCUITS LINZER

Linzer cookies originated in Eastern Europe but are enjoyed all over France come teatime. These heart-shaped and raspberry-filled cookies are perfect for Valentine's Day, but consider different shapes or even jam fillings for other holidays throughout the year.

270 g fresh raspberries

187 g granulated sugar

Juice of ½ lemon

187 g butter

100 g granulated sugar

267 g flour

14 g almond powder

2 eggs

Powdered sugar, for topping

1. Make the jam: combine raspberries and sugar in a pan and heat the mixture over low heat.

2. When it comes to a boil, turn up the heat to medium for 10 minutes and stir frequently.

3. Turn down the heat again, add the lemon juice, and let the jam reduce for 5 minutes.

4. Wait until the jam thickens (about 15 to 20 minutes total), then pour it into a glass bowl and refrigerate until it is completely cold. While the jam is cooling down, preheat the oven to 160°C/320°F and prepare your sweet dough.

5. Make the sweet dough: soften the butter and incorporate the sugar. You may use a mixer if you want.

6. Mix in the flour and the almond powder until you have a homogeneous mixture.

7. Add the eggs, one at a time.

8. Form a ball and place it in the refrigerator for at least 2 hours.

9. Roll out the dough to the thickness you desire with your rolling pin.

10. Cut shapes with a cookie cutter and place pieces on the baking sheet.

11. Bake the cookies for 15 minutes.

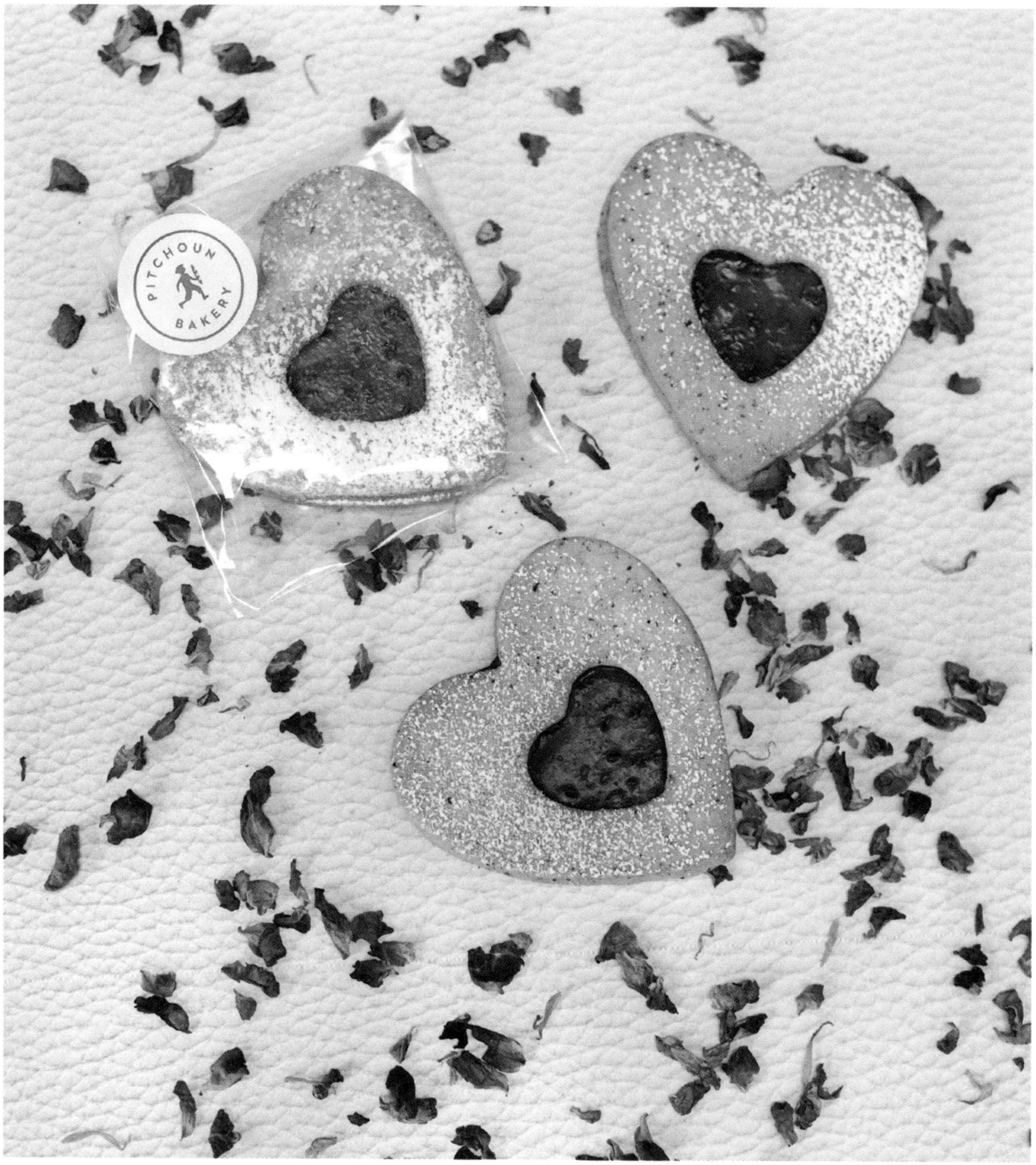

12. Once cooled, cover the cookies that will go on top when sandwiched together with powdered sugar.

13. Spread the raspberry jam with a spoon on the cookies that will go on the bottom.

14. Sandwich cookies together by placing those with powdered sugar gently on top of the jam-covered cookies.

PITCHOUN'S CRÈME BRÛLÉE

One of France's quintessential desserts is also simple—for those with a blow torch, that is. The extra tool is worth investing in to create the iconic crackled caramel crust that is as much a pleasure to break as it is to taste.

500 g heavy cream

1 vanilla bean or 10 g vanilla extract

6 egg yolks

100 g granulated sugar

50 g brown sugar

1. Preheat the oven to 160°C/320°F.

2. Pour the cream and the vanilla bean (previously split and scraped) or the extract into a saucepan. Set over medium heat and bring to a boil.

3. Once it starts boiling, remove from heat and let it rest for 15 minutes.

4. Whisk the egg yolks with the sugar until it becomes slightly white.

5. Pour the cream into the yolk/sugar mixture, stirring constantly.

6. Then pour the cream into ramekins and bake in bain-marie for 30 to 35 minutes. To bake in bain-marie, place ramekins in a large roasting pan and fill the pan with water to the halfway point of the ramekins.

7. When baked, the crèmes should be slightly golden and look cooked on the edges but still trembling in the center, like a jelly pudding.

8. Place your ramekins in the refrigerator for at least 4 hours.

9. Before enjoying your crème brûlée, spread brown sugar on top and, with a torch, melt the sugar until it becomes a caramel crispy top.

10. Now the best part is to start eating it by breaking the caramel with your spoon and enjoying the crisp as well as the smooth cream in the same bite.

CHRISTIAN REYNOSO

Christian Reynoso has been honing his skills as a chef for over a decade now in kitchens all over the Bay Area, particularly San Francisco's iconic Zuni Café. His expertise in Californian- and Mediterranean-inspired cuisine led to his now closely followed column, *Bounty*, in the *San Francisco Chronicle*. Reynoso also regularly contributes recipes and articles to NYT Cooking, *Bon Appétit*, Food52, and TASTE.

Reynoso's favorite flavors are often associated with sun-soaked regions of the world, like California and the south of France. Each recipe usually puts fresh fruit and vegetables at the forefront. This is why, for *The French Bakery*, Chef Christian has demonstrated how to prepare a classic *clafouti*, a traditional baked-custard dessert where ripened cherries are the star. A second preparation of clafouti demonstrates how this dessert can incorporate other stone fruits for an end-of-meal bite that everyone can enjoy.

CLAFOUTIS AUX CERISES

Yield: 4 to 6 servings

"Clafoutis have the unique allure of satisfying the fans of a rich and fresh seasonal-fruit, sweet ending to a meal. Custardy and full of the season's bounty, clafouti is like a fruit flan or thick fruit crêpe, simply made with a few pantry ingredients and traditionally whole, non-pitted cherries like in this recipe. Non-pitted cherries help keep the delicate cherry flavor intact and subtly perfume the cake with an almond-like flavor. Plus, having to dodge the pits makes one slow down and truly enjoy this dessert and company over conversation. However, pitted cherries are acceptable. Ideally, clafouti is served warm to lukewarm with a dusting of powdered sugar with whipped cream or vanilla-scented Chantilly cream."

—Christian Reynoso

3 tablespoons unsalted butter, melted, plus more for greasing

12 ounces whole sweet cherries, stemmed

75 g all-purpose flour

65 g granulated sugar

¼ teaspoon fine sea salt

240 g whole milk

2 large eggs

1 vanilla bean, split and seeds scraped, or ½ teaspoon pure vanilla extract

Powdered sugar, for serving

Whipped cream, for serving (optional)

1. Preheat the oven to 180°C/350°F (165°C/325°F with convection). Grease the base and sides of a 9-inch round pie dish with butter and scatter the cherries on the bottom.

2. In a medium mixing bowl, stir together flour, sugar, and salt. In a separate mixing bowl, whisk the melted butter, milk, eggs, and vanilla until well incorporated. Stir the milk mixture into the flour mixture until a smooth batter forms.

3. Pour and scrape the batter out of the bowl over the top of the cherries. Bake on the middle rack of the oven until a toothpick poked into the cake comes out clean and the top is golden, about 40 to 45 minutes.

4. Serve warm with powdered sugar over the top or with whipped cream, if desired.

CLAFOUTIS AUX PÊCHES

Yield: 4 to 6 servings

"The wide world of clafoutis starts with cherries, but those can easily be swapped out for other fruit like berries and apples or other stone fruit like slices of peaches, apricots, nectarines, and pluots. That's called being versatile and adaptable and that's a great quality in a deliciously simple and easy dessert. In this version, peaches are set in a more tangy-sweet buttermilk custard. Add a little floral saffron and buttery pistachios to top it off and this might just be a luxurious supper fit to cap off a raucous evening in the court of Versailles."

—*Christian Reynoso*

2 tablespoons unsalted butter, plus more for greasing

75 g all-purpose flour

77 g granulated sugar

¼ teaspoon fine sea salt

2 large eggs, beaten

336 g (2 cups) pitted and sliced peaches

1 teaspoon lightly packed saffron threads

240 g buttermilk

2 tablespoons raw, shelled pistachios, finely chopped, for serving

Whipped cream, for serving (optional)

Powdered sugar, for serving (optional)

1. Preheat the oven to 180°C/350°F (165°C/325°F with convection). Grease a 9-inch round pie dish, square 8-inch baking dish, or 1½- to 2-quart oval oven-safe dish. Sprinkle 1 tablespoon of sugar onto the base and walls of the dish. Scatter the peach slices in the greased dish.

2. Heat the 2 tablespoons butter in a small saucepan and, once melted, stir in the saffron threads and turn off the heat.

3. In a medium mixing bowl, stir together flour, sugar, and salt. Stir the eggs into the flour mixture until just combined. Stir the buttermilk into the melted saffron butter then pour that mixture into the flour mixture, stirring until a smooth batter forms.

4. Pour and scrape the batter out of the bowl over the top of the peaches. Bake on the middle rack of the oven until a toothpick poked into the cake comes out clean, about 45 to 50 minutes.

5. Serve warm with chopped pistachios, and optional whipped cream or powdered sugar, if desired.

DÔME AUX FRAMBOISES

True to its name, a dome dessert is a perfect half-sphere that hides layers of cake, mousse, and even jelly beneath a rounded glaze dome. This particular recipe combines rich white chocolate, tart raspberry, and delicate rose for balanced decadence in each bite.

Almond Cake

355 g cake flour

100 g almond flour

20 g baking powder

250 g egg yolks

260 g granulated sugar

225 g olive oil

450 g egg whites (about 7 to 8 large eggs)

Raspberry Gelée

500 g raspberry puree

150 g granulated sugar

4 g leaf gelatin

30 g raspberry pieces, cut small

ALMOND CAKE

1. Combine the flours and baking powder in a mixing bowl.

2. Whip egg whites in a separate bowl or mixer and add sugar in 3 stages. Whip until white and fluffy.

3. Fold olive oil into egg yolk mixture and then fold the flour mixture into the egg yolk mixture.

4. Bake in a full sheet pan for 20 to 25 minutes at 180°C/350°F.

5. Remove when center is cooked through and knife-clean.

6. Let cool before cutting out 7 cm circles.

RASPBERRY GELÉE

1. Heat 100 g of raspberry puree and sugar together in a saucepan over medium-high heat.

2. Add gelatin.

3. Remove mixture from heat.

4. Stir in remaining raspberry puree and raspberry pieces.

5. Set raspberry gelee into 6 cm molds, three-quarters full.

6. Freeze until set and ready to assemble.

Continued...

White Chocolate Mousse

140 g heavy cream

140 g milk

20 g granulated sugar

60 g egg yolks

12 g gelatin sheets

550 g Valrhona Ivoire
white chocolate

510 g heavy cream

White Chocolate Glaze

250 g milk

80 g corn syrup

8 g gelatin sheets

600 g Valrhona Ivoire
white chocolate

Organic rose petals, for garnish

Fresh raspberry, for garnish

WHITE CHOCOLATE MOUSSE

1. Bring cream, milk, and sugar to a boil.

2. Temper in egg yolks.

3. Return to a low simmer and cook to 85°C/185°F.

4. Add gelatin sheets.

5. Add white chocolate and whisk until smooth.

6. Whip cream to soft peaks and slowly fold into white chocolate.

WHITE CHOCOLATE GLAZE

1. Bring milk and corn syrup to a boil.

2. Add gelatin and white chocolate.

3. Use an immersion blender to emulsify.

4. Cool for at least 24 hours.

ASSEMBLY

1. Pour white chocolate mousse into 8 cm dome molds.

2. Insert frozen raspberry gelée disc.

3. Pour mousse to fill the dome and top with an almond cake disc.

4. Freeze domes for 24 hours.

5. Warm white chocolate glaze, unmold domes, and pour warm glaze over each dome.

6. Top with organic rose and fresh raspberry.

COUPE CHAPLAIN

French pastry shops and tea rooms offer a wide variety of ice creams, sorbets, sherbets, and other icy treats all throughout the summer months (a must for a country that doesn't care for air conditioning). Alexandra Puglisi's Coupe Chaplain hearkens to the afternoon indulgence or late-night dessert that keeps so many satisfied and refreshed—made all the better by a splash of Chartreuse.

Herb Sorbet

Yield: 3-quart sorbet

25 g cilantro

100 g basil

100 g mint

1,200 g water

320 g glucose powder

480 g granulated sugar

500 g fresh orange juice

200 g fresh lemon juice

200 g fresh lime juice

Chocolate Curls

Yield: 2 half sheet trays of curls

1 kg 66% Valrhona chocolate

HERB SORBET

1. Blanch the herbs. Set aside in the refrigerator.

2. Boil the water, glucose powder, and sugar; pour over the fresh-squeezed juices. Allow to rest overnight.

3. Using a Vitamix, blend herbs into the sorbet base, strain, and pour immediately into the ice cream machine.

4. Store in quart containers in the freezer.

CHOCOLATE CURLS

1. Temper chocolate.

2. Spread thin on acetate strips with an offset.

3. Using a chocolate comb, run along the length of the chocolate to form stripes on acetate.

4. Gently curl acetate into spirals and let crystallize overnight.

5. Peel the acetate gently off the curl and place large curls on sorbet.

ASSEMBLY

1. Add 1 or 2 scoops of herb sorbet to a plate.

2. Top with chocolate curls.

3. Add a splash of green Chartreuse to taste.

MONT BLANC

Sure, the French know that Mont Blanc is the highest peak in their country. But take a survey, and most are likely to associate the name with one of France's most beloved wintertime desserts. A Mont Blanc is a celebration of decadent chestnut cream, a particularly beloved and nostalgic French flavor, and is eaten primarily around Christmas. Alexandra Puglisi's recipe adds in orange gelée for a new spin on this classic.

Vanilla Meringue

Yield: 30 pieces

120 g egg whites

120 g granulated sugar

60 g powdered sugar

1 vanilla bean, scraped

VANILLA MERINGUE

1. Whip egg whites with 10 percent of the sugar until stiff peaks form. Add granulated sugar slowly while maintaining a stiff peak.

2. Fold the powdered sugar and vanilla bean into the meringue and pipe with an 806 tip. Yields 30 pieces.

3. Bake in a 93°C/200°F degree oven for 3 hours, or until dried all the way through.

4. Store in an airtight container at room temp.

Chestnut Cream

Yield: 2 pints

300 g chestnut pieces in syrup

150 g chestnut paste

60 g butter, softened

CHESTNUT CREAM

1. Strain chestnut pieces to get rid of excess syrup.

2. Blend chestnut pieces and paste until smooth.

3. Pass through a tamis and fold in softened butter. Store in pints.

Vanilla Chantilly

Yield: 1 pint

2 vanilla beans

1,000 g heavy cream

200 g granulated sugar

VANILLA CHANTILLY

1. Split vanilla beans lengthwise and scrape seeds from each half using the flat side of a knife. Transfer seeds to a large bowl and discard the pod.

2. Add cream and sugar, then whip ingredients together.

Continued...

Orange Gelée

Yield: 2 pints

675 g fresh orange juice

80 g granulated sugar

Zest of 4 oranges

20 g gelatin, bloomed

25 g fresh lemon juice

Fried Chestnut Chips

Yield: a few really beautiful pieces

2 fresh chestnuts

Canola oil, chilled

ORANGE GELÉE

1. Bring half the orange juice, the sugar, and orange zest to a boil.

2. Whisk in the bloomed gelatin. Pour over the remaining orange juice and lemon juice.

3. Set in a half sheet tray lined with acetate. Let set overnight.

4. Cut gelée into small squares and reserve in pints.

FRIED CHESTNUT CHIPS

1. Score the chestnuts all the way around with a paring knife.

2. Fry at 180°C to 190°C/350°F to 375°F until the shells begin to peel off.

3. Take out of the fryer and let them cool.

4. Peel the shells off and discard.

5. Take the chestnuts and mandoline them into thin pieces.

6. Add pieces to a pot of *cold* canola oil and slowly bring up to a boil. Fry chestnuts until golden brown.

7. Once desired color is reached, strain the oil. Pour onto towels to remove excess oil.

8. Reserve until plating.

ASSEMBLY

1. Using an 806 tip, pipe the chantilly onto a meringue disk, in a ratio of 3:1 cream to meringue.

2. Place the disk in the middle of a turntable, pipe the chestnut paste around the cream so as to completely hide the vanilla cream.

3. Lightly dust with powdered sugar.

4. Place on a plate of choice. Add two spoonfuls of orange gelée around the base of the meringue.

5. Garnish with a few pieces of fried chestnuts.

MATCHA COFFEE CAKE

Yield: 12 individual-sized cakes
(110 grams each)

What's more perfect for an afternoon tea than a tea-infused cake? Aya's Matcha Coffee Cake is the perfect blend of flavors, resulting in an afternoon treat that isn't overly sweet.

Cake

360 g all-purpose flour

23 g matcha tea powder

12 g baking powder

4 g baking soda

4 g kosher salt

172 g unsalted butter, softened

339 g granulated sugar

3 large eggs

5 g vanilla extract

256 g sour cream

Sesame Topping

34 g cold unsalted butter

104 g light brown sugar

50 g all-purpose flour

10 g black sesame seeds

10 g sunflower seeds

2 g kosher salt

CAKE

1. Combine and sift the flour, matcha powder, baking powder, baking soda, and salt. Set aside.

2. Place butter and sugar in a stand mixer bowl fitted with a paddle attachment. Beat on medium speed until pale (creaming method).

3. Scrape the bowl and slowly add the eggs and vanilla extract while beating on medium speed.

4. Scrape the bowl again and add the dry ingredients.

5. Beat on low speed until homogenous.

6. Scrape the bowl again and add the sour cream. Beat on low until combined.

SESAME TOPPING

1. Place all ingredients in a food processor.

2. Pulse until sandy in texture.

ASSEMBLY

1. Preheat the oven to 180°C/350°F.

2. Line a muffin pan with 12 liners and spray the liners with pan spray.

3. Divide the matcha coffee cake batter evenly into the 12 cavities.

4. On top of each cake, sprinkle a generous amount of sesame topping.

5. Bake for 12 minutes. Then rotate the muffin pan and bake for another 12 minutes.

6. Once cool to the touch, unmold from the muffin pan.

JANE THE BAKERY

Jane on Fillmore
2123 Fillmore Street
San Francisco, CA 94115

Jane the Bakery
1881 Geary Boulevard
San Francisco, CA 94115

Jane began on Fillmore Street in San Francisco in February 2011. Owner Amanda Michael opened up shop in order to provide guests with the highest quality coffee, pastries, breakfast, and lunch fare. Now, seven locations later, her mission to deliver memorable experiences to customers is an obvious success.

Amanda's decades-long career in food and hospitality inspired her to open her own establishments that focus on healthy, flavorful food made from quality ingredients. On Jane's website, Amanda's food philosophy is clearly displayed: "Here at Jane, healthy eating means having a salad and a cookie—it's all about balance."

The Jane franchise expanded in 2013 with the opening of Jane on Larkin, which introduced a line of house-made bread as well as catering services. Then, in 2016, Jane the Bakery was opened on Geary Boulevard, offering breads, viennoiseries, and pastries. Among San Francisco's many European-inspired bakeries, Jane quickly rose to the top and became known as one of the best in the city.

Amanda Michael now runs Toy Boat by Jane as well as Little Jane on Grant, and she acquired Sweet Things Bakery in Tiburon and San Francisco in November 2022.

For *The French Bakery*, Amanda provides us with a recipe for spiced gingerbread cakes called *nonettes*, which translate to "little nuns." This classic treat is often eaten during the holiday season but can be enjoyed year-round with coffee or tea. (We suggest doing so in a Jane location on a foggy San Francisco morning.)

NONETTES

Yield: 18 cakes

Nonettes

170 g honey

100 g dark brown sugar

170 g water

4 oz unsalted butter

4 g orange zest (1 orange)

204 g all-purpose flour

76.5 g rye flour or whole wheat flour

17 g Jane's Spice Blend (see below)

8 g baking powder

6 g baking soda

4 g kosher salt

1 egg yolk

26 g vanilla

Black currant jam

Jane's Spice Blend

11 g cinnamon

8 g ginger, ground

8 g allspice

6 g ground cardamom

4 g ground cloves

5 g mace

3 g ground nutmeg

3 g white pepper

These little cakes are packed with flavor from a mix of spices, and they are filled with jam. Enjoy them with coffee or tea or just on their own. This recipe uses black currant jam, but any jam or marmalade would work well. Don't skip the glaze; it adds a little extra moisture and also allows these little cakes to be good for a few days.

1. Preheat oven to 190°C/375°F and prepare the spice blend by combining all of the ingredients in an airtight jar and mixing well.

2. Grease either a mini muffin tin or a mini-cheesecake pan (see note).

3. In a saucepan over medium-low heat, combine honey, sugar, water, butter, and orange zest. Cook on low until butter and sugar have melted. Do not boil.

4. Remove from the heat and allow to cool slightly.

5. Combine flours, spice blend, baking powder, baking soda, and salt in a large bowl. Whisk well to combine.

6. Pour wet ingredients over dry ingredients and mix until just combined. Add egg yolk and vanilla and mix together.

7. Spoon batter into prepared pan. Fill each mold no more than half full. Make a small indentation with either moistened fingers or spoon and place about ¾ teaspoon jam in the indentation. Top with a small amount of batter. You want to have each mold about three-fourths full (or slightly more). The jam does not need to be completely covered.

8. Bake for about 12 minutes. The nonette should spring back slightly when gently touched. These are small and bake quickly so take care not to overbake.

Glaze

50 g powdered sugar

28 g orange or lemon juice

9. To make the glaze, combine sugar with lemon or orange juice and mix well to combine.

10. Brush with glaze while still in the pans. Let cool for about 5 minutes and remove from the pan to cool completely.

NOTE: Mini cheesecake pans are similar in size to mini muffin tins but have straighter sides, and many have the removable bottoms, which makes unmolding easier. Both work well; just be sure to grease them well.

MEG RAY

Miette
Multiple Bay Area locations

Meg Ray is the founder and owner of Miette Patisserie & Confiserie in San Francisco. She is a self-taught baker with an appreciation for French pastry and American cakes. Her recipes use organic ingredients and focus on simple, genuine flavors. She lives in Oakland and Paris and is the author of several baking cookbooks.

Miette is inspired by Parisian pastry shops, from the pale pink walls to the cakes, cookies, and pastries that line the glass display cases. The name Miette itself comes from French and means "a small crumb." Best-sellers at the bakery include macarons, chocolate éclairs, cupcakes, and cookies such as chocolate sablés.

Meg is a lifelong baker and credits being allowed to make huge messes in her childhood kitchen as an entryway into baking. But it was while traveling with her father, a NASA aeronautical engineer, to cities like London and Toulouse, France, that she discovered the charm and delicious flavors of European bakeries. When she founded Miette in 2001, it was to bring these beautiful pastries from her trips to Europe back home with her to the Bay Area.

It started with selling baked goods at the Berkeley Farmers' Market on the weekends. Within a few years, Meg opened a brick-and-mortar Miette Patisserie within the Ferry Building in San Francisco, followed by Miette Confiserie in Hayes Valley a few years later.

Miette Patisserie & Confiserie now boasts five locations throughout the Bay Area, with a new bakery slated to open in her native Oakland soon. For *The French Bakery*, Meg Ray shares her recipe for Chocolate Crème Fraîche Cake, one of her original offerings sold at the weekend farmers market. She hopes that this personal favorite will become a go-to staple for gatherings or quiet weekend indulgences.

CHOCOLATE CRÈME FRAÎCHE CAKE

"Way back when Miette was selling at the Saturday farmers market, this cake was sold as a simple loaf slipped inside a paper bag. It was easily underestimated, but the following week I'd hear its accolades from my customers. The combination of crème fraîche and cocoa powder creates an unusual flavor. It is comforting, with hints of malt and punctuated with salt and vanilla. This is not a gooey cake, and at one point we changed the name to Chocolate Bread to better set expectations. Once we moved into the Ferry Building shop, our repertoire expanded to include fancy cakes and pastries. This humble recipe got forgotten, but it has remained a personal favorite of mine. I particularly like it baked in a Bundt or kugelhopf pan and dusted with powdered sugar."—Meg Ray

200 g butter, softened, plus more for greasing

45 g cocoa powder, plus more for dusting

170 g all-purpose flour

1¼ teaspoon baking powder

¼ teaspoon baking soda

1¼ teaspoon salt

200 g granulated sugar

2 eggs, room temperature

160 g crème fraîche

1¼ teaspoon vanilla

Powdered sugar, for topping

1. Generously butter an 8-inch Bundt or loaf pan and dust with sifted cocoa powder. Sift the cocoa powder directly over the greased pan until it is completely covered. Tap out the excess.

2. Sift together the flour, cocoa, baking powder, baking soda, and salt and set aside.

3. Using an electric mixer, cream the sugar and butter until light and fluffy, about 3 minutes. Scrape down the sides of the bowl so that all the butter is incorporated.

4. Add the eggs one at a time. After both eggs are incorporated, use a spatula to scrape down the sides of the bowl until the batter is evenly blended.

5. Continue to use the spatula to fold in half of the dry ingredients.

6. Fold in the crème fraîche and vanilla, mixing until just combined.

7. Fold in the remaining dry ingredients. Mix gently but thoroughly until there are no light streaks in the batter.

8. Deposit batter into the prepared baking pan. Bake at 180°C/350°F for 40 minutes or until the top bounces back and a tester comes out clean.

9. Allow the cake to cool for 15 minus. Then tap out and allow to cool on a rack. Once completely cooled, dust with powdered sugar for decoration.

NICOLE KRASINSKI

State Bird Provisions
1529 Fillmore Street
San Francisco, CA 94115

The Progress
1525 Fillmore Street
San Francisco, CA 94115

The Anchovy Bar
1740 O'Farrell Street
San Francisco, CA 94115

Nicole Krasinksi is a renowned pastry chef as well as the co-owner of State Bird Provisions, The Progress, and The Anchovy Bar in San Francisco, along with her husband, Stuart Brioza. She and Brioza received the 2015 James Beard Award for Best Chef in the West.

State Bird Provisions was opened in the Fillmore District in 2012 and met with almost immediate accolades and success. It was named by both the James Beard Foundation and *Bon Appétit* as one of the best new restaurants in America, and was added to Zagat's ten hottest restaurants in the world list. After remodeling in 2013, it re-opened and received its first Michelin star.

In 2014 The Progress was opened in a location just adjacent to State Bird Provisions and focused on more family-style service. It also received a Michelin star in 2017. In 2020, they added The Anchovy Bar to their restaurant group.

Nicole is well known for desserts such as the ice cream sandwich at State Bird Provisions (which also features seasonal pancake stacks!). But for *The French Bakery*, she has contributed her Parsnip-Vanilla Bean Cake, a delicious, favorite mainstay on the restaurant's dinner menu.

GÂTEAU AUX PANAIS

Yield: 12 servings

"We make this cake every year for our dessert menu. The parsnips add both moisture and an earthy flavor that pairs so perfectly with the thyme and vanilla bean. We generally serve it with candied kumquats, dates, and whipped crème fraîche. But for a really standout addition we have also shaved aged gouda over the cake for a salty punch."
—Nicole Krasinski

Cake

28 g unsalted butter, for cake pan

2 large parsnips

113 g (1 stick) unsalted butter

1 thyme sprig

192 g all-purpose flour

6 g baking soda

8 g kosher salt

½ vanilla bean, split and seeded

200 g granulated sugar

2 large eggs

120 g crème fraîche, plus more, lightly whipped, for garnish

1. Preheat the oven 190°C/375°F.

2. Butter the sides and bottom of an 8-inch round cake pan.

3. Peel the parsnips and cut into 2-inch pieces. Place in a roasting pan with the 28 g butter. Cover with foil and place in the oven. Roast for 30 minutes or until the parsnips are soft.

4. Place the parsnips in a blender or food processor and blend until smooth.

5. Transfer to a bowl and allow to cool to room temperature. You need 1 cup of parsnip puree; if you have extra, save for another use.

6. If making the cake the same day, turn the oven down to 165°C/325°F.

7. Place the stick of butter and thyme in a small pan and melt over low heat. Remove from heat and set aside for 30 minutes to infuse the thyme flavor into the butter.

8. After 30 minutes, strain the butter through a fine-mesh sieve and discard the thyme.

9. In a medium bowl sift the flour, baking soda, and salt together. Set aside.

10. In a large bowl combine the butter, vanilla bean seeds, granulated sugar, and 1 cup parsnip puree.

11. Whisk together to combine.

12. Add the eggs and whisk to combine.

13. Add the sifted flour mixture and whisk to combine.

14. Add the crème fraîche and whisk to combine.

15. Pour into the prepared cake pan.

16. Bake for 45 to 55 minutes, until a cake tester comes out clean and the top is golden brown.

17. Remove from the oven and cool in the pan for 15 minutes, then transfer to a cooling rack.

18. This cake is best served the same day but can be wrapped and served the next day.

19. Cut the cake into 12 wedges and garnish with lightly whipped crème fraîche.

MARIUS DUFAY

Mirazur
30 Av. Aristide Briand
Menton, France 06500

Marius Dufay is the pastry chef at Mirazur, in Menton, France, voted the number one restaurant in the world in 2019 by The World's 50 Best and the recipient of three Michelin stars. Under the direction of Chef Mauro Colagreco, Chef Marius and team produce a fine dining experience where each recipe is developed starting in the garden before taking form on the plate. For *The French Bakery*, Marius gives us his variation on the classic fraisier cake.

MARIUS DUFAY'S FRAISIER

A fraisier is a beloved French gâteau known as much for its exquisite appearance as for its light and creamy flavor. Pastry chef Marius Dufay's version is both flourless and nut-free, making it a spring or summertime dessert for all to enjoy!

Flourless, Nut-Free Base

220 g eggs

125 g granulated sugar

75 g rice flour

60 g cornstarch

Gluten-Free Crunchy Layer

100 g brown sugar

100 g neutral oil

150 g rice flour

50 g cornstarch

3 g salt

50 g white chocolate

50 g cocoa butter

FLOURLESS, NUT-FREE BASE

1. Beat the eggs well with the sugar before sifting in the rice flour and cornstarch.

2. Spread the mixture onto a pan with a Silpat to create a very thin layer, about ⅛ inch thick.

3. Bake for 6 minutes at 180°C/350°F.

GLUTEN-FREE CRUNCHY LAYER

1. Using a mixer with a flat beater attachment, mix the brown sugar, oil, flour, cornstarch, and salt together.

2. Bake the mixture on a sheet pan at 160°C/320°F for 10 to 12 minutes.

3. Once the mixture has cooled, cut into thin strips with a knife and then, with a spatula, mix together with the chocolate and cocoa butter that have been melted together.

4. Spread the mixture onto the base in a thin layer, similar to how you would spread peanut butter onto a piece of toast. Let the whole rest in the refrigerator.

Continued...

Strawberry Insert

100 g strawberries

2 g pectin NH

15 g granulated sugar

Vanilla Mascarpone Mousse

550 g heavy cream

5 vanilla beans

110 g egg yolks

150 g granulated sugar

8.5 g gold gelatin

170 g mascarpone

Strawberry Tuile

80 g dried strawberries

280 g water

7 g cornstarch

6 g xanthan gum

19 g powdered sugar

STRAWBERRY INSERT

1. In a saucepan, heat the strawberries until they reach around 60°C/140°F.

2. Mix the pectin and sugar together and then add the mixture to the strawberries.

3. Bring to a boil and then immediately pour the mixture into a mold 1.5 inches in diameter and 1 inch deep. Place in the freezer.

VANILLA MASCARPONE MOUSSE

1. In a saucepan, add the cream. Scrape the seeds from the vanilla beans into the mixture and then add the emptied pods after. Bring the mixture to a simmer then remove from heat.

2. In a bowl, whisk together the yolks and the sugar until fully blended, then add the mascarpone. Gradually whisk the hot cream mixture into the yolk mixture (be careful to do this slowly). Add the mixture back to the saucepan and stir over low heat until the custard thickens and leaves a slight path on the back of a spoon when the finger is drawn across, about 5 minutes. Do not let the mixture boil.

3. Add the gelatin, then let the mixture rest for 12 hours in the refrigerator.

4. Mix the ingredients again with a mixer or whisk.

STRAWBERRY TUILE

1. Mix all the ingredients together in a Thermomix until mixture reaches 80°C/175°F.

2. Spread the mixture thinly over a Silpat and leave it to dehydrate overnight. (You can do this in a convection oven set at 60°C/140°F.)

STRAWBERRY CHIPS

1. Dehydrate 20 thinly cut strawberries. (You can do this in a convection oven set at 60°C/140°F.)

WHITE STRAWBERRY CARPACCIO

1. Cut 15 white strawberries (if available) into thin strips.

STRAWBERRY CARPACCIO

1. Cut 15 strawberries into thin strips.

2. If available, keep 250 g of whole wild strawberries on the side.

ASSEMBLY

1. Cut out a circle from the flourless base that is 2 inches across and put it into a cake ring that is slightly larger and 2 inches tall that has been lined with a strip of parchment paper (this will help with unmolding the dessert).

2. Place the still-frozen strawberry insert in the center of the base and add 4 g of diced fresh strawberries.

3. With the help of a piping bag, cover the entire interior of the circle with the mousse. Watch for air bubbles. Let the whole rest in the refrigerator for 12 hours. (Note from a professional: it's always better to let a fraisier rest in the refrigerator for 12 hours before tasting so that the juice from the strawberries can infuse the mousse and the magic can begin!)

4. Unmold the fraisier delicately and set it on your cake stand or plate, making sure to have removed the parchment paper.

5. Decorate the fraisier by alternating with strips of white and red strawberries, as well as the wild strawberries.

6. Now the fraisier is ready to eat!

KRISTIN BRANGWYNNE'S COCONUT STRAWBERRY PETIT GÂTEAUX

Decadent enough for a royal tea party, these coconut strawberry petit gâteaux are also sure to impress you and yours at home. The detail that truly makes these delicious small cakes stand apart? The coconut caviar that adds an extra layer of texture and illusion.

Coconut Vanilla Chiffon

385 g eggs

130 g egg yolks

385 g granulated sugar

385 g all-purpose flour

130 g butter, melted

15 g vanilla extract

35 g desiccated coconut

Strawberry Mousse

2 sheets gelatin

85 g strawberry puree

150 g granulated sugar

2 eggs

85 g butter

240 g heavy cream

Coconut Caviar

227 g simple syrup

425 g coconut puree

7 g agar-agar

COCONUT VANILLA CHIFFON

1. Combine eggs and egg yolks in a mixing bowl fitted with a whip attachment.

2. Whip eggs while gradually streaming in sugar until the mixture reaches the ribbon stage.

3. Fold in flour.

4. Fold in butter, vanilla, and coconut.

5. Spread cake batter on a Silpat-lined half sheet tray.

6. Bake at 180°C/350°F for 20 to 25 minutes, rotating once halfway through baking. Let cool before use.

STRAWBERRY MOUSSE

1. Bloom gelatin in ice water; set aside.

2. Combine strawberry puree and sugar in a pot; bring to a boil.

3. Temper strawberry mixture into eggs; return to heat and cook whisking constantly, until the mixture starts to thicken.

4. Remove from heat and stir in bloomed gelatin and butter. Set aside to cool.

5. Whip cream to soft peaks; fold into strawberry mixture.

6. Pipe mousse into desired molds. Freeze until solid.

COCONUT CAVIAR

1. Combine all ingredients in a saucepan, whisk together, and bring to a boil.

2. Boil mixture for 30 seconds.

3. Cool mixture to 60°C/140°F.

4. Drop mixture via squeeze bottle into chilled vegetable oil.

5. Strain out caviar and rinse with cold water.

ASSEMBLY

1. Unmold frozen strawberry mousse.

2. Spray mousse with pink cocoa butter spray.

3. Punch out discs of coconut sponge cake.

4. Place sprayed mousse on top of coconut cake.

5. Top with a centered pile of coconut caviar.

SIOBHAN MCKENNA

Siobhan McKenna is a baker and pastry chef currently located in Philadelphia. She got her start as a sous pastry chef for High Street Hospitality Group in Philly before moving to San Francisco to become a baker for Arsicault Bakery and sous chef at Petit Crenn in Hayes Valley.

GÂTEAU AUX CRÊPES

A spin on both traditional crêpes and crêpes cake, this version involves decadent brown butter and chocolate cream. The roasted cherries add an extra layer of sweet and just the tiniest amount of sour. It helps to make the crêpe batter and chocolate cream a day ahead so that the next day, you can cook the crêpes, roast the cherries, and build the cake.

Crêpe Batter

1 split vanilla bean

226 g unsalted butter

720 g whole milk

200 g all-purpose flour

100 g buckwheat flour

300 g eggs (6 large eggs)

40 g organic cane sugar

9 g kosher or fine sea salt

30 g melted brown butter

CRÊPE BATTER

1. Make the vanilla bean brown butter: With a small knife or paring knife, cut vanilla bean in half and scrape seeds into a small pot with butter.

2. Save scraped vanilla bean for later when roasting cherries.

3. Place the pot on medium heat and allow butter to fully melt.

4. Continue cooking until butter begins to brown and froth.

5. When butter has an amber color and has separated from the butter solids, turn off heat and keep in a place where it will stay melted if being used the same day. Can be made ahead of time, just may need to be remelted.

6. Make the crêpe batter: Scale all ingredients except brown butter into a large bowl and blend together with an immersion blender until smooth.

7. Continue to blend while streaming in melted brown butter until emulsified. Be sure to use some of the toasted brown butter solids; that's where your flavor is!

8. Allow batter to sit in the refrigerator for at least 12 hours or overnight to allow flours to hydrate and meld with the liquids.

Continued...

Chocolate Cream

180 g 64% chocolate

185 g milk

185 g heavy cream

74 g organic cane sugar

37 g egg yolk (or 2 egg yolks)

200 g heavy cream

Roasted Cherries

10 oz. fresh or frozen cherries

30 g organic cane sugar

Scraped vanilla bean saved from brown butter recipe

CHOCOLATE CREAM

1. Place chocolate in a large heat-proof bowl and set aside.

2. In a pot, combine milk, first addition of cream, and half of the sugar. Stir occasionally while bringing to a simmer.

3. In a bowl, combine yolks and remaining addition of sugar. While whisking yolk mixture, slowly stream in one-third of the hot dairy into the bowl. Pour all of this liquid back into the pot with remaining dairy.

4. Using a spatula, stir mixture along the bottom of the pot until mixture thickens and coats spatula, or until the temperature of the mixture reaches somewhere between 82°C and 83°C (179°F and 181°F).

5. Pour hot mixture into the bowl with chocolate.

6. Allow to sit for a moment to let chocolate begin to melt.

7. Whisk mixture until fully emulsified.

8. Place plastic wrap directly on top of mixture and allow to cool in the refrigerator until completely chilled and thick, at least 4 hours.

9. Once chilled, whip your second addition of heavy cream until it reaches just over medium peaks. Cream should be thick and hold its shape but still have a nice pointy peak when pulling whisk away from the bowl.

10. Gently fold cream into chocolate mixture until fully incorporated and chill again overnight in the refrigerator.

CRÊPES

1. The next day, remove crêpe batter from the refrigerator and stir to recombine ingredients.

2. Gather your vanilla brown butter and melt down again if necessary.

3. Preheat a 10-inch nonstick skillet or crêpe pan over medium heat. Use a pastry brush to lightly coat the pan with the brown butter.

4. Lift the pan from heat and ladle 2 oz. or ¼ cup batter into the center, tipping and shaking the pan so the batter covers the bottom evenly.

5. Return the pan to the stovetop and cook for about 1 minute, or until the bottom of the crêpe begins to brown and can be easily separated from the pan.

6. Using an offset spatula, lift the edges of the crêpe to loosen and slide spatula underneath to make sure it won't stick.

7. If you feel comfortable using your hands to assist the spatula, flip the crêpe over to the other side and cook for another 30 seconds until the bottom is golden brown. Remove crêpe from pan and place on a plate.

8. Continue to cook the rest of your crêpes with the remaining batter until it is gone, brushing the pan with brown butter between each crêpe. You can stack your crêpes on top of one another on the same plate until you are done.

ROASTED CHERRIES

1. Preheat the oven to 180°C/350°F.

2. If using fresh cherries, clean and remove the pits.

3. Toss cherries in sugar until evenly coated and, along with vanilla bean, place in a small roasting pan or sheet tray with edges.

4. Roast in the oven until cherry juices begin to thicken and bubble but cherries still retain their shape, about 20 minutes for fresh and closer to 30 minutes for frozen.

5. Pull from the oven and allow to cool to room temperature until ready to serve. These can also be made a day ahead and kept in the refrigerator. If doing so, briefly reheat in the oven before serving.

ASSEMBLY

1. Place one crêpe on a serving plate or cake stand. Place 2 to 3 tablespoons of chocolate cream in the center of the crêpe and spread evenly to the edges. If you leave the center of the cream slightly thinner than the edges, it will help the crêpes to stack evenly.

2. Place another crêpe directly on top of the first one, and continue to layer your cream in the same way. As your cake becomes taller, check to make sure you are stacking it evenly and adjust as needed.

3. Reserve the best-looking crêpe for the top. Place the whole cake in the refrigerator for at least 1 hour to allow the cream to set up again. This will make slicing the cake easier and ensure cleaner slices.

4. When serving, you can eat the cake chilled, but it is best at room temperature.

5. Dust the top of the cake with powdered sugar if desired, and place your roasted cherries on top. Use a large knife to cut each slice. Serve with cherries as desired.

GÂTEAU KAKI

This cake is a slight twist on a traditional coffee cake, marrying familiar flavors with the delicately sweet persimmon. A note from Siobhan: If you brew your own coffee at home, you can set aside 85 g for this recipe and reheat when ready, or if brewing an amount just for this recipe, you can use 80 g of hot water and 5 g of ground coffee. Let steep and strain out the grounds.

82 g almond flour

210 g very ripe hachiya persimmon (fuyu work too, but hachiya is best)

5 g baking soda

85 g hot brewed coffee

100 g butter, softened, plus more for greasing cake pan

95 g brown sugar

95 g organic cane sugar

100 g eggs (2 eggs)

105 g white rice flour

7 g kosher salt or fine sea salt

3 g ground cloves

Sliced almonds and powdered sugar for sprinkling on top of cake

1. Set the oven to 165°C/325°F and toast almond flour until golden in color. Set aside to cool.

2. Turn the oven up to 180°C/350°F when done.

3. Remove leaves and any seeds from persimmon and scale together with baking soda in a bowl large enough to use an immersion blender in.

4. Pour hot coffee over persimmon and baking soda.

5. Make sure to press persimmon under coffee to ensure it is all submerged. Allow to sit for at least 5 minutes to allow the baking soda and coffee to tenderize the skins of the persimmon.

6. Puree mixture with an immersion blender until as smooth as possible. Puree will thicken as it sits.

7. In a stand mixer on medium speed, cream butter and both sugars together until light in color and fluffy, about 5 minutes.

8. On low speed, add eggs one at a time and scrape down bowl and paddle in between each addition to ensure incorporation.

9. Scrape bowl and paddle again after eggs are fully incorporated.

10. Slowly add persimmon and coffee mixture until fully incorporated, scraping down bowl and paddle periodically.

11. Once incorporated, the batter will appear broken, but that's okay!

12. Whisk together almond flour, rice flour, salt, and cloves in a separate bowl.

13. Add dry ingredients to the wet mixture on low speed until fully incorporated.

14. Scrape down the bowl once more to ensure all butter and sugar haven't stuck to the bowl, and mix once more.

15. Line a 9-inch springform pan with parchment, lining both the bottom of the pan and sides. Brush the parchment lightly with soft butter.

16. Pour batter into the pan and spread out evenly to the edges.

17. Sprinkle sliced almonds on top of batter with enough to cover the surface.

18. Bake at 180°C/350°F for about 35 to 40 minutes, rotating at 20 minutes.

19. Cake is done when a cake tester comes out clean or the center of cake bounces back when slightly pressed with finger.

20. Allow cake to cool before removing sides of the springform pan and parchment. Dust cake with powdered sugar before serving and slicing.

CHAPTER 5

LES FRIANDISES

Friandise translates to "treat" and is a term that applies to any small cake or sweet. Although the French often consider a friandise to be candy, it actually pertains to any small baked good or confiserie that can be eaten by hand, usually as a snack or at the end of a meal with coffee and digestifs. Travel to a French bakery and you'll often find, among the breads and cakes, an assortment of small cakes, marshmallows, and chocolates. Purchasing such goods is a surefire way to end a dinner party right—if you can resist snacking on them on your way home.

LIANE PENSACK-RINEHART

Liane Pensack-Rinehart of Colorado Cocoa Pod actually started out her career as a software engineer. It was when she attended pastry school at Johnson & Wales University Denver and took her first course, Chocolates and Confection, that she fell in love with real chocolate. As an intern at a local chocolate shop, she also learned to paint molded bonbons. After graduating with an associate's degree in baking and pastry arts, she started Colorado Cocoa Pod in March of 2019. The idea was to create molded bonbons with flavors she had grown up with, as well as have the creative freedom in flavors and designs.

Liane currently sells online at colorado cocoapod.com and at pop-up markets and Colorado-based events as a full-time occupation. She is known for pairings, where she serves bonbons with wine, beer, bourbon, sake, and hard ciders—and often collaborates with local breweries and wineries. Her signature, however, is the Zodiac Animal Bonbon Box, which consists of twelve different bonbons, with flavors ranging from traditional to Asian-inspired, each representing one animal from the Chinese Zodiac. Her inspiration for flavor comes from desserts and Asian flavors she had growing up. Being half Chinese and half Japanese, Liane wanted to make bonbons infused with flavors from both cultures. As most Asian desserts aren't overly sweet, she also seeks to create balanced flavors with her chocolates that aren't overpowering or underwhelming.

Of course, people eat with their eyes first. So Liane always wants the colors of her bonbons to be memorable and beautiful. For *The French Bakery*, she has contributed a cranberry-orange bonbon to be enjoyed at home.

COLORADO COCOA POD'S CRANBERRY ORANGE BLISS BONBON

Yield: 32 bonbons

"Bonbons are molded chocolates that have a thin chocolate shell, a filling of ganache, caramel, praline, and/or pâte de fruit inside, and a flat chocolate bottom. They can be painted fully with colored cocoa butter, partially using the shiny tempered chocolate as a background, or without color to showcase the chocolate. The thin chocolate shell should act as a vessel to deliver the filling flavor of the bonbon, as well as help balance out the flavor and add a 'snap' texture. Bonbons can be found with traditional flavors such as sea salt caramel, milk chocolate, vanilla, etc., but I love the challenge of taking a classic or Asian dessert and putting all of that flavor into a one-to-two-bite bonbon. When people take that first bite and let the filling slowly melt on their tongue, I want them to know the flavor right away. The flavor shouldn't be overwhelming or underwhelming but the perfect bite!"

—Liane Pensack-Rinehart

Colored Cocoa Butter: Solar Flare by ChocoTransferSheets & Red Garnet by Chef Rubber

35 oz Valrhona Satilia Dark 62% (or preferred dark chocolate couverture; make sure it has a fluid rating of at least 3 drops. There will be extra; this is for shelling and capping.)

14 g (0.5 oz.) dried cranberries

14 g (0.5 oz.) candied orange peel

4.5 oz Valrhona Opalys White Chocolate 33%

14 g (0.5 oz.) vanilla bean paste

PREPPING YOUR CHOCOLATE MOLD

1. Start by making sure your polycarbonate chocolate mold is washed, clean, and dry.

2. Take a cotton pad or microfiber cloth with isopropyl and gently polish each cavity to remove any water spots or leftover colored cocoa butter.

3. Allow mold to dry and the isopropyl to evaporate.

COLORING CHOCOLATE MOLD WITH COLORED COCOA BUTTER

1. Melt colored cocoa butter according to the instructions on the bottle. Each manufacturer provides specific tempering instructions on how warm then cool their cocoa butter needs to be before using it.

2. Make sure all the isopropyl has evaporated from chocolate mold.

3. Once colored cocoa butter is in temper or cooled to around 32°C/89°F, you are ready to paint your mold.

Continued...

THIS RECIPE REQUIRES SEVERAL SPECIFIC TOOLS

- 32 cavity polycarbonate mold (using 11 g per cavity)
- Airbrush and/or paintbrush
- Isopropyl
- Cotton pads/ microfiber cloth
- Microwavable bowls

- Spatulas
- Offset spatula
- Scraper
- Piping bag
- Piping bag clip
- Parchment paper
- Thermometer
- Scale

- Gloves
- Measuring cup
- Heat gun
- Silicone mat
- Cookie sheet (optional, to place mold on top of)

---

4. Using a paintbrush, airbrush sprayer, gloved finger, or a clean cocoa butter–only sponge, paint your mold with the desired design. For this bonbon we used Solar Flare colored cocoa butter by ChocoTransferSheets sprayed into each cavity using an airbrush, then backed it with Red Garnet colored cocoa butter by Chef Rubber.

5. Make sure each cavity is covered with a thin layer of colored cocoa butter. You don't want the layer to be too thick.

6. Let mold with colored cocoa butter set up and dry in a cool area. They will be set once the colored cocoa butter is no longer shiny and the layer has turned a matte color.

SHELLING BONBONS

1. Prepare a sheet of parchment paper for tapping out excess chocolate onto.

2. Temper dark chocolate: Melt chocolate to the temperature suggested by the manufacturer. For Valrhona Satilia, heat chocolate in a small bowl in increments of 10 to 20 seconds, stirring and checking the temperature between each increment until it reads 43°C to 46°C (113°F to 115°F).

3. Cool with a few chocolate pieces, stirring until the chocolate reaches 32°C/89°F.

4. Test to make sure chocolate is in temper using a sheet of parchment paper or an offset spatula dipped in the chocolate and checking to see if it sets up within 5 minutes without any white streaks, in a matte shine.

5. Once chocolate is in temper, fill chocolate mold and push the chocolate so that it fills each cavity before scraping off the excess chocolate.

6. Gently but firmly tap the side of the mold with the bottom of your scraper or on top of the table to remove all air bubbles.

7. Turn chocolate-filled mold onto the piece of parchment and tap out all of the excess chocolate.

8. Scrape mold clean of chocolate and allow it to set up in a cool area for at least an hour before filling it.

9. Shells will start to retract. This is a good indicator that the chocolate has been tempered properly and will turn out shiny.

PREPARING FILLING

1. Roughly chop the dried cranberries and candied orange peel; set aside.

2. Melt 4.5 oz white chocolate in microwave in increments of 20 to 30 seconds, stirring between each round until completely melted. Be careful not to burn chocolate by using increments of 10 when it is 75 percent melted.

3. Heat heavy cream to at least 32°C/150°F.

4. To the melted white chocolate add the invert sugar, sorbitol, dextrose, cinnamon, ground ginger, vanilla bean paste, dried cranberries, and orange peel.

5. Slowly pour the heated heavy cream into the chocolate mix.

6. Stir slowly to combine, scraping the sides of the bowl.

7. Emulsify the mixture until smooth (30 seconds to 1 minute, scraping the sides in between).

8. Pour filling into a piping bag and cool it down by rolling it on an ice pack to 24°C to 27°C (75°F to 80°F).

FILLING YOUR BONBONS

1. Once the filling has cooled, cut off the tip of the piping bag and pipe filling into each cavity until 1 to 2 mm below the edge of the cavity.

2. Once all the cavities are filled, gently tap the mold to make sure the filling settles and evens out.

3. Allow filling to set up overnight or at least 3 hours.

CAPPING AND UNMOLDING BONBONS

1. Once the fillings have set up, temper more dark chocolate for capping.

2. Once chocolate is in temper, take a heat gun and quickly run it over the edges of the bonbons to slightly melt them. Make sure heat gun isn't too close to the mold or it could throw the chocolate out of temper.

3. Pour some chocolate over the cavities, and using a spatula or scraper, cover each cavity with a thin layer of chocolate.

4. Scrape off the excess chocolate from the mold, making the bottom of the cavities flat (best if scraped off in one try).

5. Once the chocolate starts to set up, place mold in the refrigerator for 2 to 3 hours before unmolding.

6. After the bonbons have chilled in the refrigerator, gently flex the mold and flip it over onto a silicone mat or piece of parchment.

7. Gently tap out any bonbons that don't come out immediately.

8. Allow bonbons to come to room temperature before enjoying. Keep them out of the sun and away from direct sunlight in an airtight container. Best enjoyed within 1 week.

JACOB FRAIJO AND CHRISTINA HANKS'S VANILLA CANELÉ

Yield: Twelve 80 g canelés

A canelé is a small, cake-like treat hailing from Bordeaux. Perfect at the end of a meal, preferably with coffee or a digestif, the canelé should have darkly sweet, rum-infused flavor and springy texture. This canelé recipe has been infused with vanilla to enhance your dark rum of choice. For best results, make the batter one day ahead.

92 g all-purpose flour

231 g powdered sugar

462 g whole milk

46 g unsalted butter, cubed, plus more for greasing

60 g eggs

69 g egg yolks

28 g vanilla paste or extract or ½ vanilla bean, scraped

28 g dark rum

Day 1

1. Weigh out all ingredients. Sift the powdered sugar and flour separately and set aside.

2. In a pot, bring the milk to a scald. Add the cubed butter.

3. Allow the milk to melt the butter before gently stirring to combine.

4. In a separate bowl, whisk together the eggs and egg yolks.

5. Temper with the hot milk mixture. To do this, whisk the egg mixture while slowly adding enough hot dairy to bring up the temperature of the eggs.

6. Once the egg and milk mixtures are combined, whisk in the flour slowly and gently.

7. The mixture will have lumps. Do not overmix to make the batter smooth.

8. Gently whisk in the vanilla and rum.

9. Leave in the refrigerator overnight.

Continued...

Day 2

1. When ready to bake the canelés, pull the batter from the refrigerator to temper.

2. To prep the canelé molds, lightly and evenly brush the interior with soft unsalted butter or spray them evenly with pan spray. Using a clean finger, wipe away excess spray so it is not pooled at the bottom.

3. Preheat the oven to 200°C/400°F and set the rack to the middle of the oven.

4. Gently stir the canelé batter with a spatula. Do not aerate the batter.

5. Strain the batter using a fine-mesh strainer.

6. Evenly portion the batter between the prepared molds, using up to 80 g per full-sized canelé mold.

7. Evenly space the filled molds on a flat sheet tray, ensuring there is about 2 inches between each mold.

8. Transfer the tray to the oven and set a 15-minute timer.

9. After the first timer, open the oven to let out steam. Close the oven and lower the oven temperature to 190°C/370°F for a still oven or 180°C/350°F for a convection oven. Set a second timer for 30 minutes.

10. After the second timer of 30 minutes passes, rotate the tray and allow more steam to escape the oven.

11. Close the door and set a third timer for 30 minutes.

12. At this point the canelés should be very close to having an even, dark golden color.

13. Unmold one canelé to check the color. If the color isn't even mahogany, return the canelé to its mold and continue to bake. Rotate the tray again, or as needed. Continue to check the canelés after another 5 to 10 minutes.

14. Once desired color is achieved, unmold canelés immediately onto a wire rack.

15. Allow them to cool for at least 2 hours before enjoying to ensure the custardy interior is set. Once cool, the canelés should have a thin, crisp shell and a custardy interior with an even network of holes.

CHEZ NOIR'S CANELÉ DE BORDEAUX

Beeswax Butter

Yield: 30 molds

150 g beeswax

350 g clarified butter

Canelé Batter

3 g vanilla bean

900 g whole milk

100 g heavy cream

200 g all-purpose flour

450 g granulated sugar

Pinch salt

50 g unsalted butter

140 g egg yolk

150 g rum

BEESWAX BUTTER

1. Melt the beeswax and slowly whisk in the clarified butter.

2. While still hot, brush the insides of the canelé molds with the mixture, leaving only a thin film.

CANELÉ BATTER

1. Split the vanilla bean and scrape out the seeds.

2. Combine the vanilla pod and seeds with the milk and cream. Heat the milk/cream to 80˚C/175°F. Set aside to cool.

3. In a bowl, sift the flour and combine with the sugar and salt.

4. Melt the butter and add to the flour/sugar mixture.

5. With gloves on your hands, work the butter into the mix until it's the texture of wet sand.

6. When the milk/cream has cooled to 50°C/122°F, add one-third to the flour/sugar mix and combine well. Follow by adding half of the egg/egg white mixture and mix well. Add another one-third of the milk/cream mixture and mix well.

7. Add the remaining eggs and milk and mix well.

8. Allow the batter to cool down in the refrigerator. Once cold, add the rum and mix well. Let sit for 24 hours before using.

9. The next day, bring the batter to room temperature.

10. Bake at 200°C/400°F between 30 and 50 minutes, rotating halfway through.

11. Bake until deeply caramelized.

12. Unmold right out of the oven onto a rack and let cool at room temperature.

FINANCIERS AUX OIGNONS

Yield: 28 financiers
(20 grams each)

"Guests often confuse these savory little bites for cupcakes at first glance. But don't let their cuteness fool you; they are packed with an almost umami-esque flavor and a subtle hint of sweetness. Almost as if our signature French onion soup was distilled down to one bite. These have quickly become our signature snack at The Bistro."
—Tara Gallina, co-owner of Bistro La Floraison and Take Root Hospitality

50 g almond flour

50 g all-purpose flour

25 g onion powder
(see below)

2 g baking powder

Egg whites and water

138 g ground isomalt

7 g kosher salt

94 g brown
butter, strained
and solids removed

1. Preheat the oven to 180°C/350°F.

2. In a mixing bowl, add flours, onion powder, and baking powder. Mix together and pass through a fine-mesh strainer to remove clumps.

3. In the bowl of a stand mixer, add egg whites and water and mix using the whisk attachment until stiff peaks form.

4. Switch to the paddle attachment and keep the mixer running on low while adding ground isomalt, then all remaining dry ingredients, followed by the salt. Slowly add the brown butter and mix until emulsified.

5. Place mixture into piping bags.

6. Spray baking molds with cooking spray.

7. Pipe batter into molds.

8. Bake for 10 minutes, rotate, and bake another 10.

9. Let rest until cool and remove from molds.

Gruyère Puree

Yield: more than
needed for one recipe of
financiers

300 g whole milk

3 g kappa carrageenan

100 g Gruyère

Sea salt, to taste

Sherry vinegar, to taste

GRUYÈRE PUREE

1. Add milk to a medium saucepan and heat to a simmer.

2. Whisk in kappa carrageenan for 2 minutes while milk is at a simmer.

3. Place mixture into a blender, blend on high, and add cheese until homogenous.

4. Pour mixture into a sheet pan and let cool in a refrigerator until mixture is set.

5. Cut the blocks into cubes and blend in a blender until smooth.

6. Season with salt and sherry vinegar.

7. Pass through a fine-mesh strainer. Place puree into a piping bag.

ONION POWDER

1. Thinly slice 2 yellow onions and bake in the oven overnight at 63°C/145°F until onions are dehydrated.

2. Let cool, then blend until a powder. Or you can use storebought onion powder.

GRUYÈRE CRUMBLE

1. Place shredded Gruyère onto a baking tray lined with a Silpat. Bake at 180°C/350°F for 10 to 15 minutes until cheese is golden brown and crispy.

2. Let cool. Break up the mixture into small pieces.

ASSEMBLY

1. Pipe a small amount of cheese puree on top of the financier. Make a small divot in the cheese, place a piece of thyme in the divot, and top with a small piece of Gruyère crumble.

XAVIER BAUDINET

The Grand America
555 Main Street
Salt Lake City, UT 84111

Chef Xavier Baudinet has been the executive pastry Chef for The Grand America Hotel in Salt Lake City for nine years. For *The French Bakery*, he has contributed two classic desserts, the madeleine and the macaron.

XAVIER BAUDINET'S FRENCH MADELEINES

Yield: 80 madeleines

The recipe that launched a thousand pages—or four thousand, to be exact. The madeleine is an afternoon treat made for teatime. But for the French, it is also closely associated with the writer Marcel Proust, whose epic In Search of Lost Time *begins with the protagonist biting into a madeleine and suddenly being taken back to his childhood. Une madeleine de Proust is now a common expression for anything that reminds you of your childhood. Consider yourself lucky if this perfect tiny cake was something you commonly indulged in as a child.*

9 eggs

304 g granulated sugar

380 g all-purpose flour

13 g baking soda

362 g unsalted butter, melted and cooled

50 g brown butter

50 g honey

1 g lemon zest

1. Whip together eggs and sugar until ribbon is very airy.

2. Sift flour and baking soda together.

3. Mix together flour mixture, cooled, melted butter, brown butter, and honey in stages.

4. Fold in the lemon zest.

5. Store in an insulated container or pipe and bake at 177°C/350°F until done, 10 to 12 minutes, depending on the mold.

VANILLA MACARONS

The macaron is perhaps the most Parisienne of all French baked goods. This meringue-based sandwich "cookie" with a buttercream, jam, or sometimes ganache filling is both elegant and eye-catching, colorful and subdued. Although larger versions exist, most prefer a small two-bite macaron to accompany a quick cup of coffee or tea in the afternoon—or a coupe of champagne on more festive occasions.

375 g superfine sugar

150 g water

142 g fresh egg whites

338 g almond flour (fine)

338 g powdered sugar (10x fine)

132 g egg whites

2 g vanilla bean paste

1. Scale water and caster sugar together in a pot. Scale the first part of egg whites in a clean mixing bowl with a whisk attachment.

2. Bring sugar to a boil. In the mixer, start whisking the egg whites at medium speed.

3. Increase the mixer speed to high and whisk the egg whites to a stiff peak.

4. Cook sugar to 118°C/245°F.

5. When the sugar is ready, turn down the mixer speed to medium and pour the cooked sugar gradually down the side of the mixing bowl to avoid the whisk touching the sugar.

6. Keep mixing to let it cool down and make a stiff meringue.

7. In a separate mixing bowl, scale almond flour, powdered sugar, 132 g egg whites, and vanilla paste. Combine well for a smooth paste with a paddle attachment.

8. When the meringue reaches room temperature, fold gently into the almond mix in two stages, using a rubber spatula or plastic scraper, until the mix is well combined. Do not overmix. The batter should be smooth and shiny and fall in a wide ribbon when it is lifted with a spatula.

9. Hold the pastry bag in a vertical position with one hand on the bag and the other near the pastry top to control the movement of the bag. Pipe discs about 3.5 cm/1.5 inches in diameter on parchment paper or on silicone pads.

Continued...

French Buttercream

185 g egg yolks

450 g sugar

40 g glucose syrup

60 g water

610 g unsalted
butter, softened

5 g vanilla paste

Raspberry Jam

300 g fresh raspberries

200 g raspberry puree

300 g superfine
granulated sugar

9g apple pectin

50 g freshly
squeezed lemon juice

10. Bake at 150°C/300°F for 11 to 12 minutes.

11. The next day, pair the shells and fill with desired filling.

MACARON FILLINGS

French Buttercream

1. Scale egg yolks in a mixer with whisk attachment and whip until foamy.

2. Scale sugar, glucose syrup, and water in a pot and cook until 118°C/240°F.

3. Turn the mixer to medium speed and add cooked sugar into the egg yolks.

4. When the mix is cooled close to room temperature but still slightly warm, add the softened butter in 5 stages, mixing well between each stage. Add vanilla paste to finish.

5. Add desired flavor to the buttercream and use as filling for macarons.

Raspberry Jam

1. Scale fresh raspberries and raspberry puree in a thick-bottomed pan and cook until the raspberries turn mushy.

2. Mix sugar and pectin. Add it to the raspberry mix and cook at boiling stage for 3 minutes.

3. Remove from heat and stir in lemon juice.

4. Refrigerate for 2 hours before using.

NOTE: Always use fresh egg whites. For the best texture, separate the egg whites a day before and leave them overnight at room temperature in an airtight container.

Use a digital food thermometer for the most accurate reading of sugar temperature.

For beginners, use a macaron stencil under the parchment paper to help pipe even-sized macaron shells.

METRIC CONVERSIONS

U.S. Measurement	Approximate Metric Liquid Measurement	Approximate Metric Dry Measurement
1 teaspoon	5 ml	5 g
1 tablespoon or ½ ounce	15 ml	14 g
1 ounce or ⅛ cup	30 ml	29 g
¼ cup or 2 ounces	60 ml	57 g
⅓ cup	80 ml	76 g
½ cup or 4 ounces	120 ml	113 g
⅔ cup	160 ml	151 g
¾ cup or 6 ounces	180 ml	170 g
1 cup or 8 ounces or ½ pint	240 ml	227 g
1½ cups or 12 ounces	350 ml	340 g
2 cups or 1 pint or 16 ounces	475 ml	454 g
3 cups or 1½ pints	700 ml	680 g
4 cups or 2 pints or 1 quart	950 ml	908 g

INDEX

ABOUT CIDER MILL PRESS BOOK PUBLISHERS

✳ ✳ ✳

Good ideas ripen with time. From seed to harvest,
Cider Mill Press brings fine reading, information,
and entertainment together between the covers of its
creatively crafted books. Our Cider Mill bears fruit twice
a year, publishing a new crop of titles each spring and fall.

"Where Good Books Are Ready for Press"
501 Nelson Place
Nashville, Tennessee 37214

cidermillpress.com

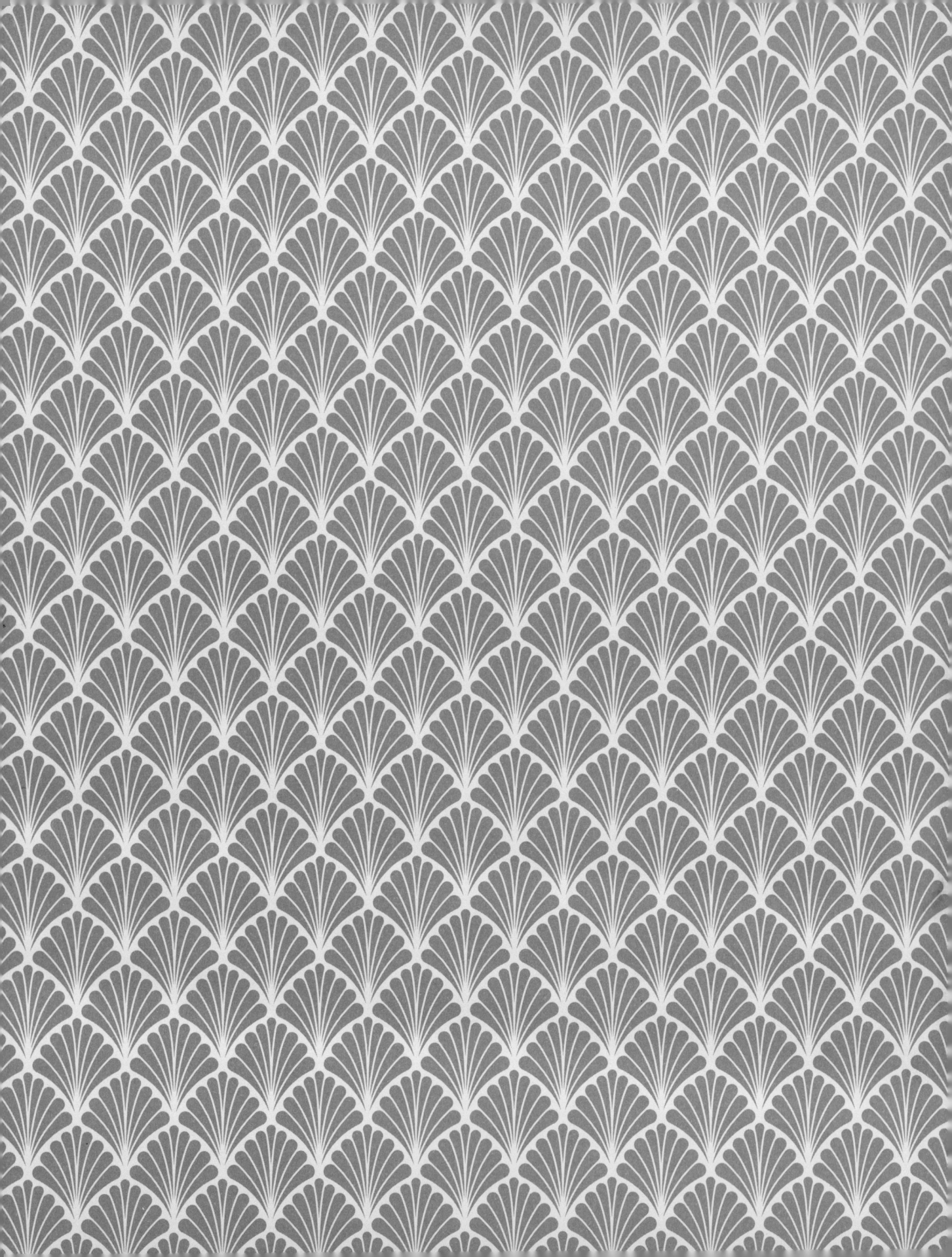